Dictionary Drills

Edward B. Fry, Ph.D.
Director, Reading Center
Rutgers University

Jamestown Publishers
Providence, Rhode Island

DICTIONARY DRILLS

**Lessons and Exercises for
Mastering Dictionary Skills**

Catalog No. 752

Copyright © 1980 by Edward B. Fry

Cover Design by Stephen R. Anthony

Printed in the United States

80 81 82 83 9 8 7 6 5 4 3 2 1

ISBN 0-89061-206-4

To the Teacher

Read the student's foreword. It gives you some indication of what these drills are about. They are not the typical class assignment in which a student is told to look up a meaning of a strange word. There is none of that in this drill book. You can make up those drills yourself if you wish. They are not necessarily bad, but they are sometimes horribly overdone and hence boring.

These drills have three purposes:

1. To acquaint the student with all the parts of the main entry. This involves word origins, parts of speech, multiple meanings, and much more.

2. To provide a thorough review of phoneme-grapheme correspondences. In elementary school, this is often called phonics; but on a more adult level, we are teaching it as a meaningful way to use the pronunciation key and to understand the phonetic part of the main entry. In fact, you can't really use the pronunciation key with any facility if you don't have at least a minimal acquaintance with English phonology and orthography. Often, even college-educated adults can stand a little brushing up in this department.

3. To show that dictionaries often contain other types of reference information, like presidential birth dates and capitals of countries.

These drills will be much more useful if you supplement them with your own knowledge. Discuss each one with your class both before and after they are done. Extend them with your own examples and drills. They are spring-boards to areas that need further teaching. For example, the drill on parts of speech provides an excellent opportunity for you to review nouns, verbs, adjectives and adverbs if you wish.

You can further extend their usefulness by showing how other dictionaries, such as *Webster's, Random House,* or *Thorndike Barnhart,* handle some of these same concepts.

Use good judgment on how far to extend the lessons. For example, an entire college course could be given on word origins. For some classes, however, just knowing that L. indicates that the word comes from Latin is enough.

The dictionary opens up the whole marvelous complexity of the English language. The purpose of these drills is to move the students ahead a notch or two, not to overwhelm them. The drills in Section II are harder than the drills in the first half of the book. Use your judgment as to when to discontinue use of the text to avoid discouraging your students.

It is our intention that this book be a unit, a part of a Reading Improvement class or a part of an English class. You are the judge of how big a part it plays. I would be pleased to receive any feedback on its usefulness, needed changes, or extensions.

In closing, I would like to thank Elaine Burgin for her editorial assistance in refining the drills in the text.

May you enjoy presenting these lessons to your classes.

EF

Contents

To the Student

If you could only use the dictionary—I mean *really* use the dictionary—you would be well on the way to better grades in school; better performance on your job; and a lifelong education. That's a pretty big promise, but it's true.

Students and employees are judged by the words they use and how they use them. If you don't use any new and difficult words, you are showing your limitations.

If you use a new word with a wrong meaning, it is a strike against you. If you mispronounce a word, it's strike two.

These drills will definitely help you to use a dictionary, almost any dictionary. We had to select one to teach with; but once you thoroughly know one dictionary, you can rapidly learn to use another. If you have never learned to use even one dictionary well, then they all will be confusing or hard to use.

We know that you have used a dictionary, or perhaps many, to look up a word meaning or to check a spelling. That is not what these drills are going to do.

These drills will help you to understand all the parts of the main entry. All the little marks and symbols will be taught and used.

If you have never studied a dictionary on an adult level before, you will be surprised at what you have to know in order to get full understanding. For example, good old "parts of speech" are used to separate meanings; word origins are used to differentiate homographs; and diphthongs are built into the pronunciation guide.

In addition, there are all sorts of other information in the *American Heritage* and other dictionaries, like the dates past presidents died, the capitals of countries, the Hebrew alphabet, the Morse code, and much more. In short, you can look up many things other than just word meanings—if you know they are there.

Some of these drills will be a review of something you were supposed to have learned earlier. But a little review is good for the memory, and it often helps improve understanding and appreciation. It is also interesting to see something you have learned elsewhere (such as phonics or grammar) applied in a useful reference work.

Most of the drills, however, will cover parts of the dictionary that are new to you. Some of these are more difficult than others, particularly those in the second half of the book concerning phonetic symbols and pronunciations. Don't be discouraged if you find the drills too hard and have to stop before completing the text. Your ability to understand the drills in Section II depends, to a great extent, on your background in phonics.

This text provides the keys which unlock the door to a wealth of information available in your dictionary. Whether you complete all or part of it, you will be rewarded every time you reach for a dictionary by your increased understanding of this useful resource.

Personal Word List

This drill will take several weeks; so get started now, and work at it as you do the rest of the drills in this book.

Add at least 5 words per week from your book or newspaper reading. Add several new words every time you do a drill.

When you come across an unknown word or a word whose meaning isn't clear to you, then enter it here under its first letter. For example, suppose you don't know the meaning of the word *levee*. Look it up in your dictionary and add the following information under the letter L:

1. The word broken into syllables
2. The phonetic pronunciation
3. The meaning

Your entry for *levee* would look like this:

L *lev·ee (lĕv′ē) An embankment raised to prevent a river from overflowing.*

9

A _____

_____

_____

_____

_____

_____

_____

_____

_____

_____

_____

B _____

_____

_____

_____

_____

_____

_____

_____

_____

C _____

_____

_____

_____

_____

_____

_____

_____

_____

_____

_____

_____

_____

D _____

_____

_____

_____

_____

_____

_____

_____

E _____

_____

_____

_____

_____

_____

_____

F _____

_____

_____

_____

_____

_____

_____

G _____

_____

_____

_____

_____

H _____

_____

_____

_____

I _____

_____

_____

_____

_____

_____

J _____

_____

K _____

_____

L _____

_____

_____

_____

_____

_____

M _____

_____

_____

_____

_____

_____

_____

_____

N _____

_____

_____

_____

O _____

_____

_____

_____

P _____

_____

_____

_____

_____

_____

_____

_____

_____

_____

_____

_____

Q _____

_____

R _____

_____

_____

_____

_____

_____

_____

_____

S _____

_____

_____

_____

_____

_____

_____

_____

_____

_____

_____

_____

_____

_____

T

U

V

W

X

Y

Z

Section 1
Understanding the Main Entry and Obtaining Reference Information

Guide Words

As you know, most reference works are organized alphabetically. By reference works we mean not only the standards like a dictionary or encyclopedia, but also many job-related reference works like telephone books, parts lists for automobiles, and ZIP Code directories.

Most reference works have guide words at the top of each page to help you locate a word or entry more quickly. Look at the guide words printed in bold type at the top of the page, at left, from the *American Heritage Dictionary of the English Language.*

Notice that the first guide word, *juice,* is the first word on the page, and the second guide word, *jurisprudence,* is the last word on the page. Because the words are listed in alphabetical order, every word on that page follows the first guide word and precedes the second guide word. So the guide words help you know at a glance if a word is on that page or not.

For example, to look up the word *jot,* you thumb through the dictionary pages until you find guide words beginning with *j.* Next, as you thumb through the pages which have guide words beginning with *j,* ask yourself, "If I put *jot* between this pair of guide words, will the three words be in alphabetical order?

Below are three pairs of guide words from your dictionary supplement.

Janus-faced / Jefferson   page 12
jigger / John   page 14
josh / jugular   page 16

Imagine *jot* between each pair of guide words. Find the series in which the words are in alphabetical order.

Janus-faced / jot / Jefferson
jigger / jot / John
josh / jot / jugular

Only the words in the last series are in alphabetical order. This tells you that *jot* must be on that page—page 16.

People who don't use guide words waste a lot of time trying to find an entry. The following drill will help you sharpen your skills in using guide words.

We will have three races of 10 words each. You can race against another person or a small group. Or, you can race against the clock to see if you can improve your time in each race. To do this, you will need to time yourself. Any watch with a sweep second hand will do.

To complete each race, you must find the dictionary page numbers for 10 words using the dictionary supplement accompanying this text. Find the page on which each word appears using just the guide words. You do not actually have to find the word itself. If the word fits alphabetically between a pair of guide words, you can be sure it is located on that page.

Example

To find the page on which *knave* appears you would do the following:

• Find the guide words beginning with *k*.

(jurist / karakul)

• Put *knave* between pairs of guide words until the result is alphabetical.

(King / knell)

• Write down the page number on which those guide words appear.

knave ___22___

There is one catch. You must have perfect accuracy or else you lose. Every page number must be correct or else you are disqualified.

Go as fast as you can, but stop after each race to rest a bit and catch your breath (and check your accuracy).

Ready? On with the first race! If you are racing against yourself, be sure to put down the starting time and ending time so that you can see how long it took you to do the first race; then, do better on the second and third races.

Drill 1

Guide Word Race

RACE 1

Starting Time:
min. _____ *sec.* _____

1. jetsam _____

2. kennel _____

3. kumquat _____

4. kiosk _____

5. jab _____

6. Johannesburg _____

7. kind _____

8. Krishna _____

9. ivory _____

10. jockey _____

Ending Time:
min. _____ *sec.* _____

Total Time: _____

RACE 2

Starting Time:
min. _____ *sec.* _____

1. lady_____

2. knee _____

3. ivy_____

4. just _____

5. krypton _____

6. juggle _____

7. karma _____

8. itself_____

9. jewel _____

10. kudos _____

Ending Time:
min. _____ *sec.* _____

Total Time: _____

RACE 3

Starting Time:
min. _____ *sec.* _____

1. kale _____

2. laminate _____

3. Krakow _____

4. knob _____

5. lair _____

6. khaki _____

7. jury_____

8. kleptomania _____

9. janitor _____

10. lag _____

Ending Time:
min. _____ *sec.* _____

Total Time: _____

Alphabetizing is the skill of putting words in alphabetical order or finding words in alphabetical order. You are called upon to use your skill at alphabetizing every time you look for a friend's name in a telephone book, use a card catalog in the library, or look for the name of a city in a map index. This is because the items in most reference materials are listed alphabetically.

One of the most frequently used reference works is the dictionary. Because all of the entries in a dictionary are listed in alphabetical order, the more you know about the rules for alphabetizing, the more efficient you will be at using a dictionary.

Finding words in alphabetical order is easier if you have a good understanding of how words are put in alphabetical order. Putting words in order is simple if the first letter of each word is different, such as *cat* and *dog*. However, when two words have several letters in common, like *intervene* and *interview*, alphabetizing becomes more difficult. You must compare the letters at the beginning of both words until you find the point where the spellings become different:

*interv*ene

*interv*iew

In this example, each word begins with the same six letters: *interv*. Therefore, the seventh letter of each word, *e* and *i*, must be used to put these two words in alphabetical order.

The process becomes more complicated when you have more than two items to alphabetize. Put the following words in alphabetical order:

manufacture _____

mailman _____

manual _____

maintain _____

The correct order is: mailman, maintain, manual, manufacture. The key to alphabetizing a series of items accurately is to take only two words at a time—and then recheck your work. Drill A will give you practice in alphabetizing words quickly and accurately.

Once you have gained skill in putting words in alphabetical order, you will find locating words in a dictionary a much easier task. There are, however, some things you should be aware of concerning the order of words in a dictionary.

In the dictionary supplement accompanying this book, all of the entries are alphabetized as if they were solid words—even if they're not. Look at the order in which the following words appear in the dictionary. They are alphabetized as if they were spelled without space between words.

air-condition	(aircondition)
aircraft	(aircraft)
Airedale	(Airedale)
air force	(airforce)

You should also know that numbers are alphabetized as if they were spelled out. Thus, to look up *4th of July*, you'd look under *f*: *Fourth of July*.

Dictionaries vary. One dictionary may follow one method for arranging the entries alphabetically while another dictionary may use a different method. The method your dictionary uses will be described in the front of the dictionary.

Practice using alphabetical order by doing the following drills. Drill A will give you a better understanding of how words are put in alphabetical order. Drills B and C will increase your efficiency at finding words in alphabetical order.

Drill 2A

Put the following words in alphabetical order.

careful	1.	_____
chipper	2.	_____
circuit	3.	_____
career	4.	_____
chorus	5.	_____
circle	6.	_____
careen	7.	_____
citizen	8.	_____
chipmunk	9.	_____
carefree	10.	_____

Drill 2B

In this drill, you should:

a. find the dictionary supplement page on which the word appears by using the guide words at the top of the page;
b. locate the exact word on the page;
c. write down the word before and the word after it;
d. draw arrows to connect the letters which were used in alphabetizing these words.

Example

Your answers should look like this:

word before   *juror*

             jury

word after   *just*

Exercise

1. word before _____

   jungle

   word after _____

2. word before _____

   kimono

   word after _____

3. word before _____

   journey

   word after _____

4. word before _____

   Kentucky

   word after _____

5. word before _____

   ladle

   word after _____

6. word before _____

   judicial

   word after _____

7. word before _____

   kernel

   word after _____

8. word before _____

   jack rabbit

   word after _____

9. word before _____

        laconic

   word after _____

10. word before _____

        keg

   word after _____

Drill 2C
Do this exercise the same way you did Drill B.

1. word before _____

        jetsam

   word after _____

6. word before _____

        jurisprudence

   word after _____

2. word before _____

        kiosk

   word after _____

7. word before _____

        knight

   word after _____

3. word before _____

        knock-knee

   word after _____

8. word before _____

        lackey

   word after _____

4. word before _____

        jonquil

   word after _____

9. word before _____

        kith

   word after _____

5. word before _____

        Juno

   word after _____

10. word before _____

        lake

   word after _____

Drill 3
Multiple Meanings
— Homographs

Sometimes when a word has two quite different meanings, the word will be listed twice in the dictionary. For example, *jumper* has two separate meanings. If you look it up in your dictionary pages, you will see the word *jumper* listed twice with a little numeral "1" after the first listing and a little numeral "2" after the second listing, like this:

jum·per¹   One that jumps.

jum·per²   A sleeveless dress worn over a blouse or sweater.

The reason the dictionary calls them different words and enters them twice is that they have different origins and different meanings. They are called *homographs,* which means they are written the same way (*homo* means "same" and *graph* means "write"). However, this does not mean that a word which is entered only once has similar meanings after it. The meanings within a single entry can be quite different, too, as we shall see later.

Drill 3

There are a number of words with multiple meanings in the dictionary pages accompanying this text. In this drill, we will give you the meaning of one of the entries. You must look up the word in the dictionary supplement to find the other entry. Then write its definition on the line provided. (If there's more than one definition, copy only the first one.) Use the guide words at the top of the page to help you locate the words.

Example

key¹   A notched metallic implement designed to open or close a lock.

key²   *A low offshore island or reef.*

Exercise

1. **jar¹**   A cylindrical glass or earthenware vessel with a wide mouth.

   jar²   _____

   _____

2. **kro·na¹**   The basic monetary unit of Iceland.

   kro·na²   _____

   _____

3. **junk¹**   Scrapped materials that can be converted into usable stock.

   junk²   _____

   _____

4. **jade¹**   Either of two distinct minerals, nephrite and jadeite, that are generally pale green or white and are used mainly as gemstones.

   jade²   _____

   _____

5. **jam¹**   _____

   _____

   jam²   A preserve made by boiling fruit with sugar.

6. **kind¹**   _____

   _____

26

kind²   A class or category of similar or related individuals; sort; type.

7. **lam¹**   To thrash; wallop.

   lam²   _____

   _____

8. **jog¹**   _____

   _____

   jog²   A protruding or receding part in a surface or line.

9. **jet¹**   _____

   _____

   jet²   A high-velocity fluid stream forced under pressure out of a small-diameter opening.

10. **kit·ty¹**   _____

    _____

    kit·ty²   A kitten or cat.

Remember to add several new words to your personal word list on pages 9 through 13 every time you do a drill; add at least five words per week from your reading.

After reading the title of this section, you may be wondering what a lesson on parts of speech is doing in a book about using a dictionary. One reason is that you won't be able to understand how meanings are arranged in your dictionary if you don't have at least a passing acquaintance with parts of speech. A second reason is that choosing the correct meaning or spelling of a word in a dictionary can depend on knowing how the word is being used—and that's what parts of speech are all about.

Knowing what part of speech a word is can be so helpful that dictionaries provide this information for almost all entries. Let's see how parts of speech are indicated in an entry. Look at the total entry for *hash*¹.

> **hash**¹ (hăsh) *n.* **1.** Chopped meat and potatoes mixed together and browned. **2.** A jumble; hodgepodge. —*v.* **1.** To chop up; mince. **2.** To discuss; go over: *hash over future plans.* [< F *hacher,* to mince.]

You will note that just after the phonetic spelling in parentheses there is a little *n.* The meanings that follow the *n.* are the meanings of *hash* when it is used as a noun. After the noun definitions there is a *v.* The meanings which follow the *v.* are meanings of *hash* when it is used as a verb. Most entries in the dictionary give the part of speech before the meaning.

In order to use this information, however, you must have at least a general understanding of parts of speech. Knowing the part of speech of a word will help you get the most out of your dictionary.

The following explanation will cover nouns, verbs, adjectives and adverbs since most of the words in the dictionary fit into these four categories. The other parts of speech are in there, but you will seldom look them up because you know them already. They are the structure words or words that hold sentences together like conjunctions (*conj.*) such as *and;* prepositions (*prep.*) such as *of;* pronouns (*pron.*) such as *he*; and interjections (*interj.*) such as *Ouch!*

Let's look at the main parts of speech:

Noun (*n.*) | The name of a person, place or thing.
Examples: mayor, city, bicycle

Verb (*v.*) | A word that shows action.
Examples: work, fall, fly

It is not always easy to determine what part of speech a word is. One problem is that a word can be a noun in one sentence but a verb in another. Look at these examples.

Noun use: | The bicycle is red.
Verb use: | You can bicycle down to the corner.

Noun use: | Zip up your fly, George!
Verb use: | Birds fly south in winter.

You can readily see that how a word is used affects its meaning—sometimes to a considerable extent (fly).

Therefore, when you want information about a word, it is not enough to know how it is spelled. You must also know which sense of the word you want to use. Then you must sort through all possible meanings until you find the one which fits the word as you're using it. Knowing whether you want a noun (*n.*) meaning or a verb (*v.*) meaning will narrow the choice and improve your accuracy.

The other parts of speech you need to know about in order to use your dictionary more effectively are adjectives (*adj.*) and adverbs (*adv.*) Briefly:

An adjective modifies a noun or pronoun.
An adverb modifies a verb.

Like nouns and verbs, whether a word is an adjective or an adverb often depends on how it is used in a sentence. For example, look at these uses of the word *quiet*.

Adjective use: It is quiet.
Adverb use: Bring it quietly.

You might note that adverbs often have an "-ly" as a suffix (a part at the end of a word).

Just to make matters a little more complicated, certain words that are adjectives or adverbs can also be used as nouns or verbs. For example:

Noun use: The quiet was welcome after the war.
Verb use: If you don't quiet that dog...

One good trick for finding out if a word is a noun is to put *the* or *a* in front of it. If it makes sense, then the word is a noun. "The box" is the name of a thing you put groceries into. A word that names something is a noun.

A good trick for finding out if a word is a verb is to put *to* in front of it. If you can, then the word is a verb. "To box" is to put something into a box. Since this is an action, "to box" is a verb.

Now that you have a working knowledge of parts of speech, the following drills will give you practice in using this information to get the most out of a dictionary.

Drill 4A

Your task is to write down the part of speech (noun, verb, adjective, adverb) for each of the definitions or word uses below.

Look up each word in your dictionary, then find the correct part of speech which applies to that particular meaning or use.

> **Example**
>
> **kick**   To strike with your foot.   _____ *verb* _____

Exercise

1. **lace**	A delicate fabric.	1.	_____
2. **lace**	To add liquor to a beverage.	2.	_____
3. **judge**	To form an opinion about.	3.	_____
4. **judge**	A public official who hears cases.	4.	_____
5. **kind·ly**	Showing sympathy or helpfulness.	5.	_____

6. **kind·ly**   In a kind way or manner.   6. _____

7. **ju·ve·nile**   Immature.   7. _____

8. **ju·ve·nile**   A young person or child.   8. _____

9. **jin·gle**   A simple, catchy rhyme.   9. _____

10. **jin·gle**   To make a tinkling or ringing sound.   10. _____

Drill 4B

Do the same thing that you did in Drill A, but use the dictionary abbreviations for the parts of speech (n., v., adj., adv.) to show your answers.

Exercise

1. **keel**   To capsize or faint.   1. _____

2. **keel**   The backbone of a ship.   2. _____

3. **just**   Precisely or exactly.   3. _____

4. **just**   Honorable and fair.   4. _____

5. **land**   To come to rest.   5. _____

6. **land**   Earth or soil.   6. _____

7. **joint**   Shared by two or more.   7. _____

8. **joint**   A point at which two or more things are joined.   8. _____

9. **know·ing**   Clever, shrewd.   9. _____

10. **know·ing·ly**   Cleverly or shrewdly.   10. _____

Accent or Stress

Dictionaries show three levels of *accent* or *stress* for the syllables in a word. The stress or accent might be thought of as the loudness with which the syllable is spoken, but it also often has something to do with the amount of time used in saying the syllable.

- The strongest accent is marked with a bold mark (′).

- The weakest accent has no mark.

- The intermediate or secondary accent is marked with a similar but lighter mark (′).

For example, in the word *jubilation,* the third syllable has the strongest accent; and the first syllable has the secondary accent. The pronunciation given in parentheses ( ) after the main entry of the word looks like this:

(jo͞o′bə-lā′shən)

You might note that the unaccented syllables contain the schwa (ə) sound. A schwa, by definition, is the unaccented vowel sound.

However, unaccented syllables do not always contain a schwa (ə); they can have any vowel sound. Look at these words. They show unaccented syllables with a long vowel sound (ē) and a short vowel sound (ĭ).

jol·ly	(jŏl′ē)
kin·dling	(kĭnd′lĭng)

It is also possible for a two-syllable word to have both a strong accented syllable (′) and a secondary accented (′) syllable. For example, the word *lactose,* a type of sugar, is pronounced (lăk′tōs′).

You might also note that the syllables are separated by hyphens (-) *or* by an accent mark, but not by both.

One-syllable words do not have any accent marks because, with only one syllable, it is the one to be stressed. For example: **keep** (kēp).

There are times when you will use a dictionary to find out how to pronounce an unfamiliar word correctly. To get the most from the dictionary pronunciation, you will need to understand the use of accent marks. Drill A will improve your skill at reading accented and unaccented syllables.

Drill 5A

Look up each word in your dictionary supplement. Write down the pronunciation, syllable by syllable, exactly as it is given within the parentheses following the main entry. Pay particular attention to the accent marks. Say the word syllable by syllable, and then as a whole word.

Example

A diamond is a *jewel.*

Jewel is pronounced __joo'əl__ . Say it. Hear the accent.

Exercise

1. He tore her new *jacket.*

   Jacket is pronounced _____ . Say it. Hear the accent.

2. The car he drives is a real *jalopy.*

   Jalopy is pronounced _____ . Say it. Hear the accent.

3. He was *jubilant* when he won the lottery.

   Jubilant is pronounced _____ . Say it. Hear the accent.

4. Did you swim in the *lagoon?*

   Lagoon is pronounced _____ . Say it. Hear the accent.

5. She is employed as a *kindergarten* teacher.

   Kindergarten is pronounced _____ . Say it. Hear the accents.

6. *Knowledge* is a valuable resource.

   Knowledge is pronounced _____ . Say it. Hear the accent.

7. The *ladybug* sat delicately upon the leaf.

   Ladybug is pronounced _____ . Say it. Hear the accents.

8. The *janitor* helped the band arrange the equipment.

   Janitor is pronounced _____ . Say it. Hear the accent.

9. The *judicial* decision was final.

   Judicial is pronounced _____ .Say it. Hear the accent.

10. A large *kangaroo* can hop along at 30 miles an hour.

   Kangaroo is pronounced _____ . Say it. Hear the accents.

Alternate Pronunciations

Many American-English words have two or more pronunciations which are proper. For example, for *jaundice,* you can say (jôn′dĭs) or (jän′dĭs). Either is correct. The one you say probably is dependent on the area of the country where you live or learned to speak.

The dictionary tends to put the most common pronunciation first, but not always.

You can call a native of Japan (jăp′ə-nēz′), or (jăp′ə-nēs′), but the dictionary saves space by not repeating syllables that are unchanged. The two pronunciations are written like this (jăp′ə-nēz′, -nēs′).

Drill 5B

Complete Drill B by writing both pronunciations in full. Then say both of them to yourself so you can hear the difference. Refer to the pronunciation key at the bottom of any pair of dictionary pages if necessary to help you pronounce the phonetic spellings. Pronunciation is taught in depth in the second part of this text.

Example

A *javelin* is a light spear.

Javelin is pronounced ___*jăv′lən*___ or ___*jăv′ə-lən*___ .

Say it both ways. Hear the difference.

Exercise

1. The *jurors* acquitted him.

   Juror is pronounced _____ or _____ .

   Say it both ways. Hear the difference.

2. *Kenya* is on the east coast of Africa.

   Kenya is pronounced _____ or _____ .

   Say it both ways. Hear the difference.

3. Piano keys are made of *ivory.*

   Ivory is pronounced _____ or _____ .

   Say it both ways. Hear the difference.

4. A *kerosene* lamp started the fire.

   Kerosene is pronounced _____ or _____ .

   Say it both ways. Hear the difference.

5. *Johannesburg* is in South Africa.

   Johannesburg is pronounced _____ or _____ .

   Say it both ways. Hear the difference.

One other type of optional pronunciation has to do with whether a Y sound should be included in the pronunciation of the word or whether it is optional.

If the Y sound is optional, it is put between diagonal lines / /. The dictionary calls these diagonal lines virgules (vûr′gyo͞ols). For example, the word *student* can be pronounced (sto͞o′dənt) or (styo͞o′dənt). The dictionary tells you this by writing the pronunciation like this: (st/y/o͞o′dənt).

When the Y sound must be included in the pronunciation, there are no diagonal lines on either side of the Y. For example, the Y sound in *beauty* must be included. Therefore, the dictionary shows the pronunciation like this: (byo͞o′tē).

Drill 5C

Look up the following words to see if the Y sound is optional or necessary. If it is optional, write /y/ on the first line and O (optional) on the next. If it is necessary, write y and N (necessary.)

Example		
studio	/y/	O

Exercise

1. jun·ior _____ _____

2. knew _____ _____

3. Jan·u·ary _____ _____

4. Ken·ya _____ _____

5. joc·u·lar _____ _____

Remember to add several new words to your personal word list on pages 9 through 13 every time you do a drill; add at least five words per week from your reading.

Drill 6
Syllabication

Syllables are interesting units. Though they can be tricky to understand, they are often helpful in sounding out new words, in learning to spell words, and in dividing a word at the end of a line.

There are two kinds of syllables. One is called *graphic syllables*. They are found in the main entry word (the first word in bold print). A centered dot is placed between syllables, like this: **ket·tle·drum.** Graphic syllables are used to divide a word at the end of a line. In general, you split the word at any syllable division.

There are, however, special rules for dividing a word at the end of a line that you should be aware of.

- Never divide a one-syllable word. Always divide words between syllables.

- Do not put a single letter of a word at the end or at the beginning of a line: **a·round, e·vent, tast·y.**

- Do not put a two-letter ending at the beginning of a line: **pay·ee, quick·en, clear·ly.**

- Do not carry forward -*ble*. If necessary, carry forward -*able* or -*ible*: **re·li·/a·ble, in·cred·/i·ble.**

- Divide hyphenated words only at the hyphen: **self-/con·fi·dence, mer·ry-/go-/round.**

The other kind of syllable is the phonetic syllable. This kind of syllable can be seen in the pronunciation of the word between parentheses immediately following the main entry: **ket·tle·drum** (kĕt′l-drŭm′). You should be familiar with phonetic syllables because we used them in the lesson on accent. Divisions are shown by either accent marks or hyphens. Phonetic syllables show you how to pronounce, rather than hyphenate, a word.

Graphic syllables and phonetic syllables are not always the same. For example, *jelly* is divided **jel·ly** graphically in the main entry, and it is divided (jĕl′ē) for pronunciation. In some words, however, the graphic and phonetic syllable divisions are very similar. For example: **lack·/lus·ter** (lăk′lŭs′tər).

Drill 6A

In Drill A, look up each word to find its graphic syllables and its phonetic syllables. See if the syllables differ.

Example

Graphic	Phonetic
jest·er	*jĕs′ tər*

Exercise

	Graphic	Phonetic
1. joker	_____	_____
2. knowledgeable	_____	_____
3. laborious	_____	_____
4. jaded	_____	_____
5. kidnap	_____	_____
6. jabber	_____	_____
7. jiffy	_____	_____
8. kennel	_____	_____
9. landing	_____	_____
10. janitor	_____	_____

One characteristic of a syllable is that it usually contains a vowel sound. An exception to
this is the syllabic /l/ and the syllabic /n/ which
form syllables by themselves (usually phonetic
syllables). For example:

la·dle   (lād′l)
Jor·dan   (jôrd′n)

But, just to keep things complicated, this
doesn't always happen. For example:

jet·ti·son   (jĕt′ĭ-sən,-zən)

Drill 6B
Below are a few words ending in /l/ and /n/ for you to look up in your dictionary. Then write
down both the graphic and phonetic syllables.

	Graphic	**Phonetic**
1. kindle		
2. jovial		
3. jerkin		
4. kitten		
5. journal		
6. kettle		
7. jiggle		
8. laden		
9. kitchen		
10. kindergarten		

Drill 7
Foreign Alphabets

You write and read the Roman alphabet. The Roman alphabet is used to write English and many other languages. It is also called the Latin alphabet because that is the language the ancient Romans spoke when they came to England 2,000 years ago.

To give you an idea of the differences in alphabets and to show you that your dictionary is also a reference work, you can have a little fun by writing your name several different ways.

Drill 7

First, find the "Table of Alphabets" in your dictionary supplement (pages 8 and 9). Use the table to do items 1, 2, 3 and 4.

1. Write your name (first and last name) in Hebrew. Note that all the vowels and a few consonants are missing; just leave them out. If you want to do it properly, write from right to left.

←

---

2. Write your name in Greek. Watch out for some differences. For example, there are different letters for long and short E and O. For /f/, use the letter *phi*. For /v/, use the letter *beta*. There is no w, but you can use the letter *upsilon*. There is no *c*, but you can use the letter *kappa* for the K sound of *c* and the letter *sigma* for the S sound of *c*. Use the letter *khi* for *ch*. Use a capital letter at the beginning of each name.

---

3. Now write your name in Arabic (Form 1). The vowels and some of the consonants are missing. (Arabic tends to be a little like Hebrew.)

_____

4. Next, write your name using the Russian alphabet. (Russian tends to be a little like Greek.)

_____

5. Now, write your name in Morse code. Look up *Morse code* in your dictionary pages (page 29).

_____

_____

6. Write the year of your birth in Roman numerals. Look up *Roman numeral* in your dictionary pages (page 32).

_____

7. Draw the hand positions for your initials in the manual alphabet used by the deaf. Look up *manual alphabet* in your dictionary pages (page 28).

Idioms and Hyphenated Words

An idiom is a phrase of two or more words which has a meaning different from the meanings of the individual words. For example, *lame duck* has nothing to do with the condition of the bird. It refers to a politician who has lost the election and is serving out the remainder of his term in office. If you were to look up the word *lame* and then the word *duck,* you wouldn't know this. Idioms are written with a space between the words, as if they were separate words, like this: *lame duck.*

However, some word combinations, probably because of frequent use, are written as one word. For example, the main entry for *landlord* is **land·lord.** Centered dots only indicate a syllable division. Hence, *landlord* is written as one word with no spaces in it.

A third option in writing English is halfway between the above two examples. This third option uses the hyphen (-) to separate two related words. For example, *land-poor* is written with a hyphen between the two words. In hyphenated words (but not idioms), the syllable divisions are also given. The main entry, then, for *jack-o'-lantern* is **jack-o'-lan·tern.**

Finally, in real-life usage in books, newspapers, magazines, signs, and personal letters, you will find some variation of use. Even dictionaries may differ. The same two words may be hyphenated, written as two separate words (an idiom), or written as a single word. When you are reading, this variation isn't a problem; but if you are a secretary typing the boss's letter, you'd better choose a single dictionary as a standard and use it if in doubt.

You must be careful, however, when you look up the spelling of a word in the dictionary. How a word is written can depend on how it is being used. For example, you *kick off* (verb) the football, but you watch the *kickoff* (noun) when the game begins.

Let's examine some words to see if they are idioms (separate words), hyphenated words, or all one word. In Drills A and B, look up each item in the left column. The words are written altogether so you won't know which form is correct. Your job is to write the words correctly as single words, hyphenated words, or separate words. Do not show syllables (ignore centered dots).

Example

jukebox _____ *juke box* _____

jackpot _____ *jackpot* _____

Drill 8A

1. jetengine ___ jet engine _____

2. knockknee ___ Knock knee _____

3. knockout (noun) ___ knockout _____

4. jawbreaker ___ jaw-breaker _____

5. justiceofthepeace ___ justice of the peace _____

6. landslide ___ Landslide _____

7. jackrabbit ___ jackrabbit _____

8. Janusfaced ___ Janus faced _____

9. keypunch ___ Key punch _____

10. jackofalltrades ___ jack of all trades _____

Drill 8B

1. kettledrum _____
2. jackknife _jack knife_____
3. knowitall _Know it all_____
4. joblot _Job lot_____
5. jackinthepulpit _____
6. lampblack _lamp black_____
7. knowhow _Know how_____
8. landgrant _Land - grant_____
9. kingpin _King pin_____
10. ivorytower _Ivory tower_____

Remember to add several new words to your personal word list on pages 9 through 13 every time you do a drill; add at least five words per week from your reading.

Two prefixes, *non-* (meaning "not") and *re-* (meaning "restoration to a previous condition") are so common and their meanings so obvious that the dictionary does not list all the words beginning with *non-* or *re-* as main entries. Instead, it lists many words beginning with *non-* and *re-* in a table following the *non-* and *re-* main entries. These tables are several pages long. If you don't know the meaning of a word in the table, you should look up the root (the word which follows *non-* or *re-*).

Drills A and B will help you become familiar with the idea that some words beginning with prefixes are main entries and some are found in tables. Look up each word and, on the line, indicate whether it is shown as a main entry or simply listed in a table.

Example

non·prof·it _*main entry*_   non·can·cer·ous _*table*_

Drill 9A

1. **non·stan·dard** _____

2. **non·com·mer·cial** _____

3. **non·at·ten·dance** _____

4. **non·skid** _____

5. **non·cit·i·zen** _____

6. **re·ap·ply** _____

7. **re·act** _____

8. **re·charge** _____

9. **re·at·tack** _____

10. **re·ac·tion** _____

11. **non·con·form·ity** _____

12. **non·sense** _____

Drill 9B

1. **non·stop** _____

2. **non·con·sent** _____

3. **non·au·to·mat·ic** _____

4. **non·sup·port** _____

5. **re·as·sign** _____

6. **re·arm** _____

7. **re·a·gent** _____

8. **non·be·ing** _____

9. **non·ob·jec·tive** _____

10. **non·com·mu·nist** _____

11. **re·ap·pear** _____

12. **re·ad·mit** _____

> Remember to add several new words to your personal word list on pages 9 through 13 every time you do a drill; add at least five words per week from your reading.

Your dictionary contains many abbreviations. They are listed alphabetically just like main entries. For example, the abbreviation for department is *dpt*. It is alphabetized as if *p* were the second letter. It follows *dozen* in the dictionary.

Like words, abbreviations sometimes mean two different things, so you have to rely on the context (where it is used) to obtain the meaning. For example, *L.* can mean either *lake* or *Latin*.

Another thing you should know is that a word can have several abbreviations. For example, *junior* can be abbreviated *Jun.* or *jun.* or *Jr.*

When the entry is an abbreviation, the dictionary gives only the full word or words which the abbreviation stands for. It does not give the meanings of the words. If you don't know what the word or words mean, look them up as main entries.

Drill 10

In this drill, your task is to look up each abbreviation in your dictionary supplement and write out the full word or words which it stands for.

Example	
La.	*Louisiana*

Exercise

1. **jct.** _____

2. **kn.** _____

3. **J.C.S.** _____

4. **L.A.** _____

5. **J.A.** _____

6. **Kr** _____

7. **J.V.** _____

8. **kt.** _____

9. **J.P.** _____

10 **lab.** _____

11. **kW** _____

12. **KP** _____

13. **K.K.K.** _____

14. **Jav.** _____

15. (Note: The abbreviation *K* can stand for four different words. Find all four.)

a. **K** _____

b. **K** _____

c. **K** _____

d. **K** _____

Remember to add several new words to your personal word list on pages 9 through 13 every time you do a drill; add at least five words per week from your reading.

Etymology (ĕt′ə-mŏl′ə-jē) is the history of a word or the study of word origins. In your dictionary pages, the etymologies of most words are shown in brackets [ ] after the definitions. Look at the entry for *kinetic*.

> **ki•net•ic** (kĭ-nĕt′ĭk) *adj.* Of or produced by motion. —*n.* **kinetics** *(takes sing. v.).* **1.** The study of all aspects of motion, comprising both kinematics and dynamics. **2.** The study of the relationship between motion and the forces affecting motion. [Gk *kinētikos* < *kinein*, to move.]

The etymology first lists the language of origin. *Gk,* the abbreviation for *Greek,* indicates that *kinetic* comes from the Greek language.

Next the etymology lists the word that *kinetic* comes from. *Kinetic* is derived from the Greek word *kinētikos.*

Following *kinētikos* is the symbol < . This symbol means "from." According to the etymology, then, *kinetic* is derived from the Greek word *kinētikos* which comes from an earlier Greek word, *kinein.*

An etymology also tells what the word of origin means. The meaning of *kinein* is "to move."

Now look at one of the entries listed above *kinetic.* Read its etymology.

> **kin•e•mat•ics** (kĭn′ə-măt′ĭks) *n.* *(takes sing. v.).* The study of motion exclusive of the influences of mass and force. [< Gk *kinein,* to move.] —**kin′e•mat′ic, kin′e•mat′i•cal** *adj.* —**kin′•e•mat′i•cal•ly** *adv.*

Kinematics is also derived from the Greek word *kinein.* Notice the relationship between the meaning of the word of origin, "to move," and the meaning of the modern word *kinematics,* "the study of motion." Likewise, *kinetic* means "of or produced by motion," *kinetics* is "the study of all aspects of motion," and *kinesthesia* is "the sensation of bodily movement." All of these words have the same etymology. Hence, they all have to do with motion.

Recognizing the etymology of an unfamiliar word can give you insight into its meaning. For example, look at the word *hyperkinetic.* A knowledge of prefixes would tell you that *hyper-* means "great amount or excess." You know that *-kinetic* comes from the Greek word for motion. *Hyperkinetic,* then, has something to do with an excess of motion. A *hyperkinetic* child is one who has an abnormal amount of bodily movement.

A knowledge of word origins can increase your vocabulary many times over. If you know that the Greek word *kinein* means "to move," you have the key to deciphering all of the words in our language which are derived from it. You can build a knowledge of word origins by studying ancestor languages, such as Greek or Latin. Or you can build word knowledge simply by developing the habit of reading the etymology whenever you look up a word in the dictionary.

Drill 11A

Drill A will help you understand the abbreviations used for the language of origin in an etymology. You know that *Gk* stands for *Greek*. Latin may be indicated by one of several abbreviations: *L,* Latin; *LL,* Late Latin; *VL,* Vulgar Latin; and *NL,* New Latin. A complete list of abbreviations and symbols used in the etymologies is shown in your dictionary supplement on page 7. Turn to this page and find each abbreviation listed below. On the lines provided, tell what the abbreviations mean.

Example

OE *Old English*

Exercise

1. **Heb** _____

2. **F** _____

3. **G** _____

4. **Afr** _____

5. **Mex** _____

6. **Sw** _____

7. **Tag** _____

8. **Ar** _____

9. **Russ** _____

10. **Yidd** _____

Drill 11B

Drill B will give you experience with word origins in full. Look up the etymology for each main entry and write it on the line provided. (Write out the name of the language of origin; do not use the abbreviation.)

Example

1. **jar¹** *[<Arabic jarrah, large earthen vase.]*

Exercise

1. **knit** _____

2. **lamp** _____

3. **ken·nel** _____

4. **lad·en** _____

5. **kryp·ton** _____

6. **ju·ry** _____

7. **kale** _____

8. **jet·ty** _____

9. **ken** _____

10. **ju·bi·lee** _____

Remember to add several new words to your personal word list on pages 9 through 13 every time you do a drill; add at least five words per week from your reading.

Most of the time, we read words; but many times, we read symbols. Symbols are often used in traffic signs, mathematics, and in many other fields.

Drill 12A

A general set of symbols can be found in your dictionary supplement beginning on page 33. Turn to that page and find each symbol listed below. On the lines provided, write the meaning of each symbol.

Example	≠ _____ *not equal to* _____

Exercise

1. ∞ _____

2. Σ _____

3. ℞ _____

4. # _____

5. @ _____

6. © _____

7. ∠ _____

8. ∴ _____

9. ·· _____

10. ♀ _____

Drill 12B

Write the symbol for each of the following words or phrases.

1. greater than _____

2. because _____

3. plus or minus _____

4. gas _____

5. divided by _____

6. logical sum _____

7. per cent _____

8. equiangular _____

9. minus _____

10. less than _____

Remember to add several new words to your personal word list on pages 9 through 13 every time you do a drill; add at least five words per week from your reading.

Drill 13
Reference

The whole idea behind reference works is that you can't know or remember everything there is to know. A dictionary is a reference work (or book) in which you can find word meanings, proper spelling, and many other kinds of useful information. Nobody knows all the words in the English language. That is why everybody needs a dictionary.

Get the dictionary habit by looking up the meaning and pronunciation of strange words, arguing about word meanings with your friends, looking at word origins, and writing down words that are new to you in a "personal dictionary" or word list. You will find that the size of your vocabulary will grow significantly. This will help you to read different or more difficult material. It will help you to read even ordinary things like newspapers and magazines with more understanding, and it will help you to get better scores on civil service, employment, or higher education entrance examinations.

The dictionary supplement accompanying this book is from an abridged, or shortened, dictionary. An abridged dictionary contains many thousands of words, but not all words. Larger dictionaries, called unabridged dictionaries, have many more words. If you look up a word and can't find it in a small dictionary, go to a larger one.

There are many types of reference works besides dictionaries. There are encyclopedias, which have articles on a wide variety of topics; the thesaurus, which gives clusters of related words; books of maps (atlases); books which list the title and author of every book in print; books which list basic facts in medicine, chemistry, and practically any field you can name. All libraries have a reference section which has many of these books, and the librarian can help you find them. In fact, there are even reference librarians who can tell you where to find the answer to a wide variety of questions. If you want to know anything, just ask; the service is usually free.

For certain kinds of basic reference information, however, your dictionary may be the place to start. Drills A and B will help you become familiar with the kinds of information available in a dictionary.

Drill 13A

There are many famous people listed in a dictionary. They are entered alphabetically according to their last names (or single names, as in the case of a king or ancient person). The entry gives you the full name, date of birth and death, and what the person did or is most noted for. Answer the questions below by looking up the person's name in your dictionary supplement.

1. Who was Kublai Khan's grandfather? _____

2. Who was Andrew Johnson? _____

3. When was Martin Luther King, Jr., born? _____

4. When did Thomas Jefferson die? _____

5. What was Juno's husband's name? _____

6. Which President of the United States was Andrew Jackson? (number) _____

7. In which war was Lafayette a leader of American troops? _____

8. What nationality was Kepler? _____

9. When was Lyndon Johnson born? _____

10. Who was Ben Jonson? _____

Drill 13B

A dictionary also has geographical information. Answer each question by looking up the country, city, or other geographical name.

1. What countries border on Kenya? _____

2. What is the capital city of Kenya? _____

3. How many people live in Jerusalem? _____

4. Lagos is the capital of what country? _____

5. What page contains a map of the Ivory Coast? _____

6. The kip is the basic money unit of what country? _____

7. What is the capital of Jordan? _____

8. In which sea is Jamaica located? _____

9. Khartoum is the capital of what country? _____

10. What is the population of Lahore? _____

Section 2
Using the Pronunciation Key

Take a look at your dictionary supplement. After every word (main entry), you will see in parentheses the word respelled phonetically. In some words, the phonetic spelling is identical or very similar to the word; for example, *jam* (jăm). In other words, however, it is very different; for example, **jai a•lai** (hī′lī′). The key to the sounds is given by key words written across the bottom of any two facing dictionary pages.

Left-hand Pages

ă pat/ā ate/âr care/ä bar/b bib/ch chew/d deed/ĕ pet/ē be/f fit/g gag/h hat/hw what/ ĭ pit/ī pie/ ĭr pier/j judge/k kick/l lid, fatal/m mum/n no, sudden/ng sing/ŏ pot/ō go/

Right-hand Pages

ô paw, for/oi boy/ou out/o͝o took/o͞o coo/p pop/r run/s sauce/sh shy/t to/th thin/*th* the/ ŭ cut/ûr fur/v van/w wag/y yes/z size/zh vision/ə ago, item, edible, gallop, circus/

This section of the book will teach you to use this key more effectively. It will also help you to sound out unfamiliar words even without the aid of a dictionary when you are using a telephone book, a map, or other reading materials in which you find unfamiliar words.

We will begin with the consonants. They have few variations, and the pronunciation key has very few changes or different symbols for them. An understanding of consonant sounds will give you the background you need for later, more difficult, lessons.

Pronouncing some consonants in isolation is not as easy as it seems. With the consonants, you should avoid making a schwa /ə/ sound whenever possible. A schwa /ə/ sound is a soft short sound (UH) heard at the beginning of *ago*. Also, when pronouncing some sounds, such as /t/, you should avoid using your "voice" or vocal cords.

Practice saying the twelve most common consonants given on the next page. You should say each word slowly and carefully, concentrating on the sound of each beginning consonant. Most of them sound the way you would expect them to sound. However, there are some things you should be aware of when practicing each sound. Guidelines for pronouncing each sound are shown in parentheses after each example.

Now practice making the twelve consonant sounds aloud. Read each example and the guideline in parentheses. Refer to the box for an explanation of the guideline. Then read the example again. Go over the list twice forward and twice backward so that you can rapidly make each sound in isolation.

Guidelines

(t)	A single consonant within parentheses means it is a stopped sound—it can't be sustained.
(voiceless)	If the consonant is "voiceless," it is made with the breath only; do not use your vocal cords.
(rrr)	Repeating the consonant means that the sound can be sustained.
(də)	If a schwa /ə/ sound (UH sound) is needed, it is given. If not, don't add a schwa sound.

1. T as in Top (t voiceless)
2. R as in Ring (rrr)
3. D as in Dog (də)
4. N as in Nut (nnn)
5. M as in Man (mmm)
6. S as in Saw (sss voiceless)
7. L as in Letter (lll)
8. P as in Pencil (p voiceless)
9. F as in Fish (fff voiceless)
10. C as in Cat (k voiceless)
11. B as in Book (bə)
12. V as in Valentine (vvv)

Drill 14A

Two of the twelve letters which you practiced above represent two sounds. The letter S may have an S sound, as in _saw,_ or it may have a Z sound, as in _was._

The letter C sometimes makes the K sound, as in _cat,_ or it may make the S sound, as in _city._ Hence, in the pronunciation key, there is no _c_ because it really has no sound. Sometimes it is /s/ (the S sound) and sometimes /k/ (the K sound).

In this drill, indicate the sound made by the letter S in each word by writing either /s/ or /z/ on the line provided. Say the sound as you write it.

Example

sa_t_ _____/s/_____   ha_s_ _____/z/_____

Exercise

1. eye_s_ _____
2. _S_am _____
3. plea_s_ant _____
4. _s_andpaper _____
5. be_s_t _____
6. famou_s_ _____
7. hi_s_toric _____
8. ea_s_e_____

9. pa_s_try _____
10. _s_alary _____
11. rea_s_on_____
12. M_s._ _____
13. _s_cale _____
14. wa_s_te_____
15. pre_s_ent _____

Drill 14B

Indicate the sound made by the letter C in each word by writing either /k/ or /s/ on the line provided. Say the sound as you write it.

1. corridor _K_____

2. factual _____

3. uncanny _____

4. sauce _____

5. copyright _____

6. bacteria _____

7. graceful _____

8. placement _____

9. fraction _____

10. incident _____

11. nicotine _____

12. suffocate _____

13. sacred _____

14. instructor _____

15. comparison _____

Short and Long Vowels

Vowels are the letters A, E, I, O, U, and sometimes Y. One way they differ from the consonants in the last lesson is that they all have two or more sounds.

The two most common sounds are the *short* sound and the *long* sound. For example, the letter O has the short sound in the word *ox* and the long sound in the word *no*. Say these words to yourself, and pay attention to the two sounds the letter O makes.

The pronunciation key at the bottom of each pair of pages in your dictionary supplement tells you whether the vowel is short or long by putting diacritical marks above the vowel like this:

ŏx (short)   nō (long)

Drill 15A

Put the proper diacritical mark above the *o* in each of the following words. Do not pay attention to any other letters. Just mark the *o's*.

Example		
	drŏp	jōke

Exercise

1. not
2. home
3. hot
4. stop
5. hope

6. pop
7. alone
8. so
9. clock
10. hello

Drill 15B

The letter A has the short sound in the word *at* and the long sound in the word *ate*. Mark the short and long *a's* in the following words. Mark only the *a's*.

Example		
	ăt	āte

Exercise

1. had
2. back
3. made
4. baby
5. as

6. after
7. radio
8. last
9. able
10. and

Drill 15C

The letter E has the short sound in the word *end* and the long sound in the word *he*. Mark the short and long *e's* in the following words. Mark only the *e's*.

Example		
	ĕnd	hē

Exercise

1. egg
2. she
3. extra
4. be
5. then

6. get
7. legal
8. rebound
9. equal
10. edit

Drill 15D

The letter I has the short sound in the word *is* and the long sound in the word *fire*. Mark the short and long *i's* in the following words. Mark only the *i's*.

Example		
	ĭs	fīre

Exercise

1. into
2. five
3. if
4. inch
5. ride

6. did
7. this
8. tiny
9. which
10. pilot

Drill 15E

Some dictionaries use /ū/ to indicate a long U sound. However, the *American Heritage Dictionary* does not have a long sound for the letter U. It handles the sound at the beginning of a word like *use* with a /y/ and a /ōo/. Hence, *use* is spelled phonetically like this: /yōoz/.

The letter U has the short sound in the word *up*. Mark the short *u's* in the following words so you will become familiar with this sound in the pronunciation key.

Example	
	ŭp

Exercise

1. us
2. under
3. but

4. run
5. much
6. just

Drill 16
Rules for Long Vowels

You know that vowels are sometimes short and sometimes long. The problem in sounding out a new word is, "When is the vowel short and when is it long?"

Sometimes the only way to know is to look up the pronunciation of the word in your dictionary. There are some rules, however, which may help you.

Open-Syllable Rule

If a syllable ends in a vowel, that vowel is often long. There is also a closed-syllable rule which states that if a syllable ends in a consonant, the vowel is often short.

Example

nō   nō•tion   *BUT*   nŏt   nŏv•el

Drill 16A

Determine if the vowel in each word is short or long by applying the open-syllable rule. Put a short mark (˘) over the short vowels and a long mark (−) over the long vowels.

1. so

2. hot

3. fox

4. clock

5. go

6. drop

Final E Rule

An *e* at the end of a word often makes the vowel long. This is sometimes called the "final *e* rule." To be more precise, an *e* at the end of a word containing another vowel is silent, and it usually makes the other vowel long.

A third way of stating this is that in a "pattern" of **CVCe** (**C**onsonant + **V**owel + **C**onsonant + **e**), the vowel is long.

Example

nŏt   nōt̸ͤ

Drill 16B

Determine if the vowel sound in each word is short or long by applying the final *e* rule. Put a short mark over the short vowels and a long mark over the long vowels. If the *e* is silent, put a slash (/) through it: nōt̸ͤ.

1. hot

2. body

3. home

4. joke

5. stop

6. stone

7. globe

8. pop

9. mat

10. mate

11. like

12. did

Drill 16C:
Review

Determine if the vowel sound in each word is short or long by applying both the open-syllable rule and the final e rule. Put a short mark over the short vowels and a long mark over the long vowels. Put a slash through an *e* that is silent, but *only* if it is silent. An *e* may be short, long or silent.

If the vowel is long, write which rule the word follows: "open-syllable" or "final *e*." If it is short, write "closed syllable."

Example

hē _____ *open-syllable* _____

rōsé _____ *final e* _____

lĕft _____ *closed-syllable* _____

Exercise

1. up _____

2. nose _____

3. she _____

4. came _____

5. white _____

6. egg _____

7. last _____

8. five _____

9. bit _____

10. bite _____

11. go _____

12. be _____

13. lone _____

14. stash _____

15. mom _____

16. pope _____

17. sup _____

18. hi _____

19. dot _____

20. pole _____

Y Rules

- A *y* at the beginning of a word makes its consonant sound.

  yes   (y**ĕ**s)

- A *y* at the end of a one-syllable word makes a long I sound.

  m**y**   (m**ī**)

- A *y* at the end of a word usually makes a long E sound if it is the second vowel sound.

  iv**y**   (**ī**'v**ē**)

Drill 16D

Indicate which sound the *y* in each word makes by writing / y / or /ī/ or /ē/ on the line provided.

Example

yarn __/y/__

fly __/ī/__

baby __/ē/__

Exercise

1. any _____

2. you _____

3. only_____

4. year_____

5. sky _____

6. youth _____

7. lady_____

8. yawn_____

9. navy _____

10. cry_____

11. yellow_____

12. try_____

13. flaky _____

14. young _____

15. crafty _____

16. by _____

17. yen _____

18. vestry _____

19. why _____

20. lofty _____

72

Difficult Consonants

In this lesson, we will cover the remaining consonant sounds and see how they are usually spelled. We will also learn how they are represented in the phonetic pronunciation system of the *American Heritage Dictionary*.

The dictionary pronunciation symbol is shown between slash lines. In some cases, the symbol is the same as the letter; but in other cases, it is quite different. Let's look at the easy ones first—those with no change.

Consonants *H, K, W* and *Z*

      H as in *hat* is /h/ (h voiceless)
      K as in *king* is /k/ (k voiceless)
      W as in *wag* is /w/ (www)
      Z as in *zebra* is /z/ (zzz)

Pronounce the beginning consonants, below left, three times each.

The Consonants *X* and *Q*

There are two consonants that really don't have any sound of their own, the letter X and the letter Q. The letter X is usually pronounced /ks/ at the end of a word like *box*. The letter Q usually appears with a letter U, as in *queen*. Together, they are pronounced /kw/.

Drill 17A

Look up the following words in your dictionary supplement, and write down the phonetic spelling of each one next to the word. The phonetic spelling is shown in parentheses right after the entry. Remember to add the short vowel mark (˘ called a *breve*) and the long vowel mark (¯ called a *macron*) above the vowels when you copy the phonetic spelling.

On the next line at right, write the dictionary pronunciation symbol for the X or Q sound.

Example

box bŏks x /ks/

Exercise

1. **jon•quil** ______ qu ______
2. **jinx** ______ x ______
3. **kum•quat** ______ qu ______
4. **jux•ta•pose** ______ x ______

The Consonant *G*

The consonant G has two sounds. The letter G makes a regular sound, /g/ as in *gate;* it also makes a J sound, /j/ as in *giant.* The letter G is usually read /g/ before *a, o* and *u;* it tends to be pronounced /j/ before *i, e* and *y.* Knowing this will help you pronounce unfamiliar words.

Drill 17B

Drill B will help you remember when to pronounce the letter G /g/, and when to pronounce it /j/. It is also a review of the consonants X and Q.

Write the dictionary pronunciation symbol /g/, /j/, /kw/, or /ks/ after each of the following words to indicate the sound made by the underlined letters.

Example

queen /kw/

ago /g/

gem /j/

fix /ks/

Exercise

1. ox ______
2. quart ______
3. large ______
4. change ______

5. six _____

6. page _____

7. dog _____

8. next _____

9. quit _____

10. tax _____

11. equal _____

12. age _____

13. quote _____

14. go _____

15. gave _____

16. bridge _____

17. gone _____

18. quake _____

19. maximum _____

20. gumbo _____

21. lax _____

22. giant _____

23. aqua _____

24. gin _____

Consonant Digraphs

There is another group of consonant sounds which is sometimes called consonant digraphs because they are written with two letters. The word part *di-* means "two," and *graph* means "write." In the dictionary, three of the digraphs have pronunciation symbols written exactly as they are spelled:

CH as in *chair* is /ch/ (ch voiceless)
SH as in *shoe* is /sh/ (sh voiceless)
TH as in *three* is /th/ (th voiceless)

Pronounce the above digraphs three times each.

Let's look at another sound made by the digraph TH. The TH sound in *them* is not the same as the TH sound in *three*. Say *them* and *three* slowly to yourself, emphasizing the first part of the word. The TH sound in *them* is voiced—you use your vocal cords when you make the sound. It is really a different sound, and dictionaries give it a different pronunciation symbol. The *American Heritage Dictionary* uses the symbol /th/ for this sound of TH. Note that this voiced TH symbol has a slant to it. Look at the pronunciation key at the bottom of any odd-numbered dictionary page, and note the way the two TH digraphs are written phonetically.

Finally, the last digraph is really a blend; that is, it is two sounds together. The WH sound as in *wheel* is pronounced /hw/. The /h/ comes first, then the /w/.

Drill 17C
Write the dictionary pronunciation symbol for each of the following words to indicate the sound made by the underlined letters.

Example

thin _____ /th/ _____

mother _____ /th/ _____

she _____ /sh/ _____

when _____ /hw/ _____

chair _____ /ch/ _____

Exercise

1. the _____

2. thank _____

3. they _____

4. such _____

5. both _____

6. show _____

7. what _____

8. fish _____

9. teach _____

10. other _____

11. while _____

12. cheer _____

13. father _____

14. ninth _____

15. ship _____

16. awhile _____

17. there _____

18. chunk _____

19. where _____

20. wish _____

21. than _____

22. bishop _____

23. much _____

24. think _____

Drill 18
Schwa and Long Vowel Digraphs

The Schwa Sound

The schwa is the unaccented vowel sound which can be represented by the letters: *a* (*a*gain), *e* (happ*e*n), *i* (rec*i*pe), or *o* (gall*o*p). It is sometimes described as the sound made by a person trying to lift something very heavy.

It is represented in your dictionary supplement by /ə/.

The schwa is an unaccented vowel sound, which means that there is always another accented vowel in the word.

Drill 18A

In each of the following words, the letter which stands for the schwa sound is left out. Fill in the blank with *a, e, i* or *o.* Check your dictionary supplement if you're not sure.

1. jew ___ ler

2. kang ___ roo

3. judici ___ l

4. j ___ lopy

5. k ___ bob

6. lam ___ nate

7. jabb ___ r

8. jamb ___ ree

9. lab ___ r

10. jovi ___ l

11. kin ___ scope

12. l ___ crosse

The schwa sound /ə/ can be contrasted with the short sound of the vowel. Remember, in the *American Heritage Dictionary* the short sound of *e,* as in *red,* is marked with a little curved line (breve) over the letter /ĕ/. If you need to review the short vowel sounds, look back at Drills 15 and 16.

Drill 18B

On the line following each word, write either the schwa symbol, /ə/, or the short vowel symbol, /ă/, /ĕ/, /ĭ/, /ŏ/ or /ŭ/, for the underlined vowel.

Example

<u>a</u>gain	/ə/	<u>a</u>t	/ă/
happ<u>e</u>n	/ə/	r<u>e</u>d	/ĕ/
rec<u>i</u>pe	/ə/	<u>i</u>s	/ĭ/
gall<u>o</u>p	/ə/	<u>o</u>x	/ŏ/

Exercise

1. <u>a</u>lone _____

2. cl<u>o</u>ck _____

3. <u>A</u>meric<u>a</u> _____

4. childr<u>e</u>n _____

5. <u>a</u>fter _____

6. sec<u>o</u>nd _____

7. leath<u>e</u>r _____

8. qu<u>i</u>t _____

9. r<u>a</u>g _____

10. p<u>e</u>t _____

Long Vowel Digraphs

Vowel digraphs are two-letter combinations that make the long vowel sound of the first letter. They are listed below with examples of each:

        long E /ē/ **EA** in read (rēd)
        long E /ē/ **EE** in feet (fēt)

        long A /ā/ **AI** in paid (pād)
        long A /ā/ **AY** in play (plā)

        long O /ō/ **OA** in boat (bōt)
        long O /ō/ **OW** in own (ōn)

There is only one problem with these vowel digraphs: two of them also make another sound.

        OW also makes the /ou/ sound as in *now.*
        EA also makes the /ĕ/ sound as in *bread.*

Drill 18C

This drill will help you learn the pronunciation symbols for these vowel digraphs as they are used in the *American Heritage Dictionary*. On the line following each word, write the dictionary pronunciation symbol for the underlined letters.

Example

feet _____ /ē/   boat _____ /ō/

read _____ /ē/   own _____ /ō/

bread _____ /ĕ/   now _____ /ou/

paid _____ /ā/   play _____ /ā/

Exercise

1. ahead _____   16. plow _____

2. easy _____   17. soap _____

3. thee _____   18. steady _____

4. rain _____   19. green _____

5. may _____   20. strait _____

6. breakfast _____   21. repeat _____

7. wheel _____   22. mayor _____

8. tail _____   23. gray _____

9. throw _____   24. heavy _____

10. eagle _____   25. feet _____

11. chain _____   26. coat _____

12. always _____   27. east _____

13. road _____   28. loan _____

14. slow _____   29. yellow _____

15. cow _____   30. allow _____

Drill 18D:
Review

This drill is a review of all the vowel sounds discussed in this lesson. On the line following each word, write the dictionary pronunciation symbol for the underlined vowel or vowel digraph. Use the information in the box to help you.

Schwa Sound			Vowel Digraphs		
a	again	/ə/	ee	feet	/ē/
e	happen	/ə/	ea	read	/ē/
i	recipe	/ə/	ea	bread	/ĕ/
o	gallop	/ə/			
			ai	paid	/ā/
Short Vowels			ay	play	/ā/
a	at	/ă/	oa	boat	/ō/
e	red	/ĕ/	ow	own	/ō/
i	is	/ĭ/	ow	now	/ou/
o	ox	/ŏ/			

Exercise

1. veteran _____
2. mop _____
3. brow _____
4. player _____
5. mechanical _____
6. pest _____
7. mellow _____
8. reason _____
9. leave _____
10. pat _____
11. maid _____
12. clearance _____
13. tree _____
14. ship _____
15. offend _____

16. arithmetic _____
17. throat _____
18. clipper _____
19. incredible _____
20. tray _____
21. economy _____
22. town _____
23. jabber _____
24. Pacific _____
25. instead _____
26. grow _____
27. governor _____
28. boxing _____
29. bead _____
30. get _____

Drill 19
R-modified Vowels

When the letter R follows a vowel, the vowel sound is neither long nor short. Teachers sometimes prefer to call these "R-modified vowels." Look at the R-modified vowels and the pronunciation symbols used in your dictionary supplement:

- The letter combinations ER, IR and UR all tend to make the same sound: *her, sir, fur.* The dictionary pronunciation symbol for this sound is /ûr/. The symbol ^ is called a *circumflex.*

- The letter combination OR is pronounced like the *or* in *for.* Its dictionary pronunciation symbol is /ôr/.

- The letter combination AR has two sounds: /är/, as in *far,* and /âr/, as in *care.* The symbol ¨ is called a dieresis (dī-ĕr′ə-sĭs).

Drill 19A

Write the dictionary pronunciation symbols for the R-modified vowels in the words below.

Example				
h<u>er</u>	/ûr/	f<u>or</u>	/ôr/	
s<u>ir</u>	/ûr/	f<u>ar</u>	/är/	
f<u>ur</u>	/ûr/	c<u>are</u>	/âr/	

Exercise

1. f<u>ir</u>st _____

2. w<u>ere</u> _____

3. st<u>ar</u> _____

4. f<u>or</u>th _____

5. f<u>ir</u> _____

6. c<u>ur</u>l _____

7. M<u>ar</u>ch _____

8. aw<u>are</u> _____

9. n<u>or</u>th _____

10. r<u>are</u> _____

11. d<u>ir</u>t _____

12. m<u>ore</u> _____

13. v<u>ar</u>y _____

14. c<u>er</u>tain _____

15. <u>ar</u>my _____

16. h<u>ar</u>d _____

17. g<u>ir</u>l _____

18. l<u>or</u>d _____

19. M<u>ar</u>y _____

20. h<u>ur</u>t _____

Drill 19B:
Review

This drill is a review of R-modified vowels and long vowel digraphs. On the line following each word, write the dictionary pronunciation symbols for the underlined letters. Use the information in the box to help you.

R-modified Vowels			Long Vowel Digraphs		
er	h<u>er</u>	/ûr/	ea	r<u>ea</u>d	/ē/
ir	s<u>ir</u>	/ûr/	ee	f<u>ee</u>t	/ē/
ur	f<u>ur</u>	/ûr/	ai	p<u>ai</u>d	/ā/
or	f<u>or</u>	/ôr/	ay	pl<u>ay</u>	/ā/
ar	f<u>ar</u>	/är/	oa	b<u>oa</u>t	/ō/
ar	c<u>ar</u>e	/âr/	ow	<u>ow</u>n	/ō/

Exercise

1. t<u>ur</u>key ——————————

2. <u>ar</u>tist ——————————

3. <u>ea</u>ch ——————————

4. <u>er</u>mine ——————————

5. g<u>oa</u>l ——————————

6. p<u>ur</u>ple ——————————

7. can<u>ar</u>y ——————————

8. <u>ar</u>m ——————————

9. str<u>ee</u>t ——————————

10. b<u>ir</u>th ——————————

11. <u>or</u>der ——————————

12. aw<u>ay</u> ——————————

13. sn<u>ow</u> ——————————

14. th<u>ir</u>sty ——————————

15. secret<u>ar</u>iat ——————————

16. j<u>ai</u>l ——————————

17. Th<u>ur</u>sday ——————————

18. <u>ar</u>e ——————————

19. sh<u>ar</u>e ——————————

20. det<u>er</u>mine ——————————

This sound is fairly simple. It consists of one sound with four ways to spell it. We call this the "broad O" sound (though not everybody else does). First, the broad O sound is made by the letter O in *cost*. The *American Heritage Dictionary* pronunciation symbol for it is /ô/.

The same sound is made by the letters AL, as in *all*. It is also made by the letters AW, as in *saw,* and AU, as in *auto*. The symbol for all of these sounds is /ô/.

Demonstrate your understanding of the above paragraphs by writing the correct dictionary pronunciation symbol for the vowel sounds in the following words:

c<u>o</u>st _____

c<u>a</u>ll _____

j<u>aw</u> _____

h<u>au</u>l _____

You should have written the symbol /ô/ after each of the above words because the vowel sound is the same even though the spelling of the sound is different. Look up the phonetic spelling of *jaw* in your dictionary supplement. (The phonetic spelling is found in parentheses after the entry.) Notice how the *aw* is represented.

Let's review the sounds the letter O can make.

- The letter O can make a short O sound: /ŏ/ as in *ox*.

- The letter O can make the broad O sound: /ô/ as in *cost*.

- In unaccented syllables, it can make the schwa sound: /ə/ as in *gallop*.

- The letter O makes a long sound

    when it is followed by a consonant and a silent E: /ō/ as in *home;*

    when it is at the end of a syllable: /ō/ as in *no;*

    when it is part of the vowel digraphs OA and OW: /ō/ as in *oak* and *own.*

Drill 20:
Review

The letter O represents many sounds. For each word below, decide if the underlined letter (or letters) makes the short O sound (/ŏ/), the broad O sound (/ô/), the schwa sound (/ə/), or the long O sound (/ō/). Indicate your answer by writing the dictionary pronunciation symbol on the line provided. Use the information in the box to help you.

	Short O Sound			Long O Sound Final E Rule	
o	ox	/ŏ/	o	home	/ō/
o	mop	/ŏ/	o	mope	/ō/
o	not	/ŏ/	o	note	/ō/
	Broad O Sound			**Open-Syllable Rule**	
o	cost	/ô/	o	no	/ō/
al	call	/ô/	o	stereo	/ō/
aw	jaw	/ô/	o	over	/ō/
au	haul	/ô/	o	local	/ō/
	Schwa (UH) Sound (in an unaccented syllable)			**Long Vowel Digraphs**	
			oa	boat	/ō/
o	gallop	/ə/	oa	oak	/ō/
o	second	/ə/	ow	low	/ō/
o	offend	/ə/	ow	own	/ō/
o	observe	/ə/			

Exercise

1. awful _____

2. blow _____

3. second _____

4. radio _____

5. coat _____

6. straw _____

7. wrote _____

8. bowl _____

9. author _____

10. box _____

11. original _____

12. stone _____

13. road _____

14. lawn _____

15. pot _____

16. fall _____

17. cause _____

18. open _____

19. mom _____

20. globe _____

21. show _____

22. zero _____

23. drop _____

24. sodium _____

25. somber _____

Remember to add several new words to your personal word list on pages 9 through 13 every time you do a drill; add at least five words per week from your reading.

Drill 21

Diphthongs and Review of **A** Sounds

The letter combinations OU, OW, OI, and OY are called "diphthongs" (dĭf'thôngs'). A diphthong is a type of vowel sound which is made by sliding from one vowel sound to another. Or some people would say a diphthong is a vowel plus a semi-vowel (extra half vowel).

The OU and OW Diphthongs

The *American Heritage Dictionary* pronunciation symbol for both the OU and OW diphthongs is /ou/. These diphthongs sound the same. It is the sound made by OU in *out* and by OW in *how*.

You may remember OW from Drill 18. There we discussed the long O sound (/ō/) that the letter combination OW sometimes makes, as in *own* or *know*. You can consider the /ou/ sound of OW as in *now* to be its second sound.

The OI and OY Diphthongs

There is another diphthong made by the letters OI and OY as in *point* and *boy*. The phonetic symbol for this sound is /oi/.

Drill 21A

Write the dictionary pronunciation symbol for each of the following words.

Example		
ou̱t	/ou/
o̱wl	/ou/
o̱il	/oi/
to̱y	/oi/
kno̱w	/ō/

Exercise

1. jo̱y _____

2. vo̱ice _____

3. o̱ur _____

4. allo̱w _____

5. so̱und _____

6. destro̱y _____

7. lo̱w _____

8. po̱ison _____

9. bro̱wn _____

10. lo̱yal _____

11. flo̱wer _____

12. fello̱w _____

13. co̱in _____

14. o̱unce _____

15. emplo̱y _____

16. amo̱unt _____

17. cho̱ice _____

18. cro̱wd _____

19. tomorro̱w _____

20. fo̱und _____

Drill 21B:
Review

This drill will serve as a review of the sounds made by the letter A. For each word, decide whether the underlined letter (or letters) makes a short A sound (/ă/), a long A sound (/ā/), the schwa sound UH (/ə/), or the R-modified vowel sounds (/är/ or /âr/). Use the information in the box to help you.

Short A Sound			Long A Sound Final E Rule		
a	at	/ă/	a	ate	/ā/
a	pan	/ă/	a	pane	/ā/
a	glad	/ă/	a	glade	/ā/

Schwa (UH) Sound (in an unaccented syllable)			Open-Syllable Rule		
a	ago	/ə/	a	ba•by	/ā/
a	America	/ə/	a	ca•ble	/ā/
a	again	/ə/	a	gla•cier	/ā/

R-modified Sound of A			Long Vowel Digraphs		
a	far	/är/	ai	paid	/ā/
ar	army	/är/	ai	daisy	/ā/
ar	care	/âr/	ay	play	/ā/
ar	canary	/âr/	ay	always	/ā/

Exercise

1. flavor _____   6. hate_____

2. same _____   7. thousand _____

3. Sam _____   8. train _____

4. crazy_____   9. today _____

5. hat_____   10. fullback _____

11. tom<u>a</u>to _____

12. f<u>ar</u>m _____

13. <u>a</u>nnouncer _____

14. ch<u>ai</u>n _____

15. ma<u>g</u>azine _____

16. w<u>a</u>ry _____

17. m<u>ai</u>l _____

18. <u>a</u>way _____

19. st<u>a</u>re _____

20. <u>a</u>rc _____

Remember to add several new words to your personal word list on pages 9 through 13 every time you do a drill; add at least five words per week from your reading.

Open your dictionary supplement to any right-hand page. In the pronunciation key at the bottom, you will see /o͝o **took**/ and /o͞o **coo**/. These are two different sounds which are often made by the letter U or by other letters.

Read the examples at right and say each word carefully to yourself. Note the vowel sound in each and contrast the two sounds.

| /o͝o/ | took | bull | foot |
| /o͞o/ | moon | blue | food |

Drill 22A

In this drill, indicate which OO sound is used in each of the following words. Write either /o͝o/ or /o͞o/ on the line after each word.

1. crook _____

2. full _____

3. soon _____

4. loop _____

5. suit _____

6. sugar _____

7. hook _____

8. sue _____

9. brute _____

10. wood _____

Drill 22B

Write either /o̅o̅/ or /o͞o/ following each of these words.

1. pull _____

2. loose _____

3. cool _____

4. choose _____

5. put _____

6. wolf _____

7. maroon _____

8. super _____

9. bullet _____

10. flew _____

The two sounds /o̅o̅/ and /o͞o/ are sometimes confused with other vowel sounds, particularly sounds made by the letters O and U. Read the examples at right. Listen for the different sound each makes.

/o̅o̅/	/o͞o/	/ŭ/	/ûr/	/ō/
look	moon	cut	fur	go
pull	true	just	her	own

Drill 22C

Write the correct dictionary pronunciation symbol for the vowel sound heard in each of the following words. It will be only one of the five given above.

1. bush _____

2. goose _____

3. urge _____

4. new _____

5. up _____

6. soon _____

7. blew _____

8. slow _____

9. move _____

10. book _____

11. word _____

12. tooth _____

13. woman _____

14. nut _____

15. shoot _____

Finally, /o͞o/ sometimes has the letter Y in front of it. For example, the verb *use* is spelled phonetically (yo͞oz) to show that it sounds different from *ooze* (o͞oz).

Drill 22D

In this drill, indicate whether you hear just the regular /o͞o/ or a /yo͞o/ by writing either pronunciation symbol after each word.

1. united _____

2. brutal _____

3. screw _____

4. fuse _____

5. booze _____

6. fume _____

7. soon _____

8. chew _____

9. fuel _____

10. goof _____

Remember to add several new words to your personal word list on pages 9 through 13 every time you do a drill; add at least five words per week from your reading.

Drill 23
Consonant Blends and Phonograms

Knowing how to use the dictionary pronunciation key is a valuable dictionary skill. It will help you use your dictionary quickly and effectively. It also has an important fringe benefit. Understanding a dictionary pronunciation key is closely related to phonics skill which enables you to sound out unknown words. This is called word attack skill. It is a very valuable skill to have because nobody, not even the best readers, knows all the words in the English language. When you are reading and come across a strange word, it will be easier for you to learn it if you can say it with some approximation of correctness. Skill in word attack can help you say the word aloud correctly.

In this lesson, you will learn two elements commonly used as part of word attack skills.

Consonant Blends

Consonant blends are usually two consonants which appear together and are sounded closely together, like the ST in *stop* or the GR in *grass*. Blends do not appear in the pronunciation key because a letter sounds the same in a blend as it does by itself. However, it helps readers of unfamiliar words if they see the two letters as a unit and sound them as a unit rather than as individual letters.

Phonograms

Another word attack element that good readers use is the phonogram. A phonogram is a group of letters consisting of vowel and consonant sounds that form a part of a word. For example, the letters OP form a phonogram that can be seen in many words, like *mop, hop, stop, crop,* and so on.

Thus, with this type of phonogram, a single consonant sound or a consonant blend can be added to form new words. Or, going the other way, if you know the sound of the blend CR and you know the sound of the phonogram OP, you can easily put them together to hear the word *crop* even though you might not have seen or heard the word before.

Drill 23

In each item, combine the initial consonant sounds with the phonogram to form three words. Then, using the list of consonant sounds on page 100, see how many more words you can make up using that phonogram. Write them down on a separate sheet of paper.

Example

-ide

s _____ *side* _____

sl _____ *slide* _____

r _____ *ride* _____

On a separate piece of paper, write as many *-ide* words as you can using the list of consonant sounds. Here are some examples:

hide	bride	stride
tide	pride	chide
wide	glide	

Use a dictionary if you are in doubt as to whether the combination is a word or if you are unsure of the spelling.

One real problem is that when you write some words phonetically, they sound correct but aren't spelled correctly. For example, *fride* sounds correct, but it is spelled *fried*. Avoid writing down words which sound correct phonetically but should be spelled another way.

Exercise

1. -ick

   s _____

   st _____

   p _____

3. -ight

   f _____

   s _____

   sl _____

2. -ought

   b _____

   th _____

   f _____

4. -ound

   s _____

   f _____

   gr _____

5. -ore

s _____

m _____

st _____

6. -atch

c _____

h _____

th _____

7. -ock

r _____

s _____

d _____

8. -old

f _____

m _____

s _____

9. -eak

bl _____

sp _____

str _____

10. -ack

sn _____

p _____

r _____

11. -ip

h _____

sn _____

dr _____

12. -ob

s _____

r _____

kn _____

13. -oop

l _____

c _____

tr _____

14. -ow

sl _____

kn _____

t _____

Consonant Sounds

Here is a list of consonants, blends and digraphs to help you write extra words on a separate sheet of paper for each of the preceding fourteen phonograms.

Single Consonants	Consonant Blends
b	br
c	cr
d	dr
f	fr
g	gr
h	pr
j	tr
k	
l	
m	sc
n	sk
p	sm
qu	sn
r	sp
s	st
t	sw
v	
w	bl
x	cl
y	fl
z	gl
	pl
	sl

Consonant Digraphs	
	tw
th	
sh	
ch	scr
wh	str

Remember to add several new words to your personal word list on pages 9 through 13 every time you do a drill; add at least five words per week from your reading.

The *ZH* Sound

One sound in the *American Heritage Dictionary's* pronunciation key is the ZH sound that is heard in the middle of a word like *vision*. It does not occur too frequently, but it is a sound sometimes used in English. It is not a blend, and it usually is spelled with the letter S, but not always, as in the word *garage*.

The *PH* Sound

The letter combination PH makes the F sound, as in *telephone*.

The *NG* Sound

Perhaps you wondered why your dictionary supplement has the letter combination NG in the pronunciation key. The answer is that this combination is not a blend, but a unique sound (phoneme) such as is made by other letters in the key. If you would like to prove to yourself that it is not a blend (in which each letter is pronounced), say the word *no* slowly, and note your tongue position as you say the letter N.

Now, say the word *sing* slowly; note that your tongue never gets into the N position.

Silent Letters

There are some letter combinations in English which regularly have a silent letter or letters. These are the most common ones:

KN The K before N is silent: *knife*.

WR The W before R is silent: *write*.

GH The two-letter combination GH is usually silent: *right*.

CK The C before K is silent: *back*.

E Perhaps you will remember from Drill 16 that the letter E at the end of a word is often silent and usually makes the preceding vowel long, as in *make,* but not always, as in *some*.

In Drills A and B, indicate which sound is made by the underlined part of each word using the pronunciation symbols shown below.

/zh/   vision

/f/   phone

/ng/   sing

/—/   Use a dash for any silent letter, such as:

K before N, as in knife

W before R, as in write

GH, as in right

C before K, as in back

E at the end of a word, as in make

Example

photo _____ /f/ _____   wrong _____ /—/ _____

bring _____ /ng/ _____   bought _____ /—/ _____

Exercises

Drill 24A

1. physician _____

2. know _____

3. stick _____

4. bang _____

5. measure _____

6. young _____

7. might _____

8. leisure _____

9. wrap _____

10. tale _____

Drill 24B

1. pleasure _____

2. come _____

3. trick _____

4. wrench _____

5. eight _____

6. knot _____

7. television _____

8. stuck _____

9. graphite _____

10. knoll _____

11. trea<u>s</u>ure _____

12. belo<u>ng</u> _____

13. <u>w</u>restle _____

14. crim<u>e</u> _____

15. stu<u>ng</u> _____

16. lu<u>c</u>k _____

17. <u>k</u>nock out _____

18. <u>ph</u>antom _____

19. <u>w</u>rite _____

20. fri<u>ght</u> _____

Remember to add several new words to your personal word list on pages 9 through 13 every time you do a drill; add at least five words per week from your reading.

Comparing Other Dictionary Phonetic Systems

In previous lessons, you have learned how to use the pronunciation key in the *American Heritage Dictionary*. Each dictionary, such as *Webster's, Random House,* and so on, has its own kind of pronunciation key. No two are exactly alike. However, if you know how to use any one of them, you can rapidly learn to use any of the others.

In this lesson, you will learn about two other widely used dictionary systems: the *Merriam Webster* (there are other kinds of *Webster* dictionaries) and the *Thorndike Barnhart*.

Let's look at a few of the differences.

Short Vowel Markings

One major difference between the *American Heritage* and the other two systems is that the other two do not mark short vowels with a breve (˘). Notice these differences in the chart below.

Sounds of OO

Each of the other systems uses a one-dot U, /u̇/, and a two-dot U, /ü/, instead of the short OO, /o͝o/, and the long OO, /o͞o/. Study the examples in the chart.

The Schwa

The *Webster* system is a little more liberal in its use of the schwa symbol, /ə/. It is even used in place of the short U symbol /ŭ/. In the *American Heritage*, the schwa is used for the UH sound in unstressed syllables: ago /ə-gō′/; the short U symbol /ŭ/ is used for stressed syllables.

More Differences

The chart on pages 106 and 107 gives all the symbols as they differ from the *American Heritage* system. The symbol used by both *Webster* and *Thorndike Barnhart* is the same as that used by the *American Heritage* unless a different symbol appears in the chart. The dash (—) means no change from *American Heritage*.

	American Heritage	Webster (Merriam)	Thorndike Barnhart
Short Vowel Markings			
p<u>a</u>t	/ă/	/a/	/a/
p<u>e</u>t	/ĕ/	/e/	/e/
p<u>i</u>t	/ĭ/	/i/	/i/
p<u>o</u>t	/ŏ/	/ä/	/o/
c<u>u</u>t	/ŭ/	/ə/	/u/
Sounds of OO			
t<u>oo</u>k	to͝ok	tu̇k	tu̇k
b<u>oo</u>t	bo͞ot	büt	büt

Sample Word	American Heritage [Houghton Mifflin]	Webster (Merriam) [American Book Co.]	Thorndike Barnhart [Scott, Foresman]
p<u>a</u>t	ă	a	a
p<u>ay</u>	ā	—	—
c<u>are</u>	âr	eər	er, ar
f<u>a</u>ther	ä	—	—
<u>b</u>i<u>b</u>	b	—	—
<u>ch</u>ur<u>ch</u>	ch	—	—
<u>d</u>ee<u>d</u>, mille<u>d</u>	d	—	—
p<u>e</u>t	ě	e	e
b<u>ee</u>, prett<u>y</u>	ē (prĭt'ē)	—	—
<u>f</u>i<u>f</u>e, <u>ph</u>ase, rou<u>gh</u>	f	—	—
<u>g</u>a<u>g</u>	g	—	—
<u>h</u>at	h	—	—
<u>wh</u>ich	hw	—	—
p<u>i</u>t	ĭ	i	i
p<u>ie</u>, b<u>y</u>	ī	—	—
p<u>ier</u>	îr	iər	ir
<u>j</u>u<u>dg</u>e	j	—	—
<u>k</u>i<u>ck</u>, <u>c</u>at, pi<u>que</u>	k	—	—
<u>l</u>id, need<u>le</u>	l (nēd'l)	—	— (nē'dl)
<u>m</u>u<u>m</u>	m	—	—
<u>n</u>o, sudde<u>n</u>	n (sŭd'n)	—	—
thi<u>ng</u>	ng	—	—
p<u>o</u>t	ŏ	ä	o
t<u>oe</u>	ō	—	—

Sample Word	American Heritage [Houghton Mifflin]	Webster (Merriam) [American Book Co.]	Thorndike Barnhart [Scott, Foresman]
c<u>au</u>ght, p<u>aw</u>, <u>or</u>der, <u>all</u>	ô	ȯ	—
n<u>oi</u>se	oi	ȯi	—
t<u>oo</u>k	o͝o	u̇	u̇
b<u>oo</u>t	ō͞o	ü	ü
<u>ou</u>t	ou	au̇	—
<u>p</u>o<u>p</u>	p	—	—
<u>r</u>oa<u>r</u>	r	—	—
<u>s</u>au<u>c</u>e	s	—	—
<u>sh</u>ip, di<u>sh</u>	sh	—	—
<u>t</u>ight, stopp<u>ed</u>	t	—	—
<u>th</u>in	th	—	—
<u>th</u>is	*th*	<u>th</u>	ŦH
c<u>u</u>t	ŭ	ə	u
<u>ur</u>ge, t<u>er</u>m, f<u>ir</u>m, w<u>or</u>d, h<u>ear</u>d	ûr	ər	ėr
<u>v</u>al<u>v</u>e	v	—	—
<u>w</u>ith	w	—	—
<u>y</u>es	y	—	—
<u>z</u>ebra, <u>x</u>ylem	z	—	—
vi<u>s</u>ion, plea<u>s</u>ure, gara<u>ge</u>	zh	—	—
<u>a</u>bout, jew<u>e</u>l, ed<u>i</u>ble, gall<u>o</u>p, circ<u>u</u>s	ə (unstressed syllable)	—	—
butt<u>er</u>	ər (unstressed syllable)	—	—
<u>u</u>se, f<u>ew</u>	yō͞o	yü	yü
<u>au</u>nt	ă, ä	a, ȧ	a

Note: Dash (—) means no change from *American Heritage*.

Adapted from the *American Heritage Dictionary of the English Language* (© 1973 by Houghton Mifflin Company), *Webster's New Elementary Dictionary* (© 1977 by G. & C. Merriam Co.), *Thorndike Barnhart Advanced Dictionary* (© 1974 by Scott, Foresman and Company)

Drill 25A

Write the phonetic spelling of each word in the phonetic systems of three different dictionaries: the *American Heritage* system, which you already know, and the two new systems, *Webster* and *Thorndike*. Try to write the *American Heritage* phonetic word from memory. The chart will show you the differences between the three systems.

Example

	American Heritage	*Webster*	*Thorndike*
jewel	jōo′əl	jü′əl	jü′əl

	American Heritage	*Webster*	*Thorndike*
1. fowl	_____	_____	_____
2. back	_____	_____	_____
3. jug	_____	_____	_____
4. juicy	_____	_____	_____
5. share	_____	_____	_____

Now correct your answers to be sure you are on the right track. Then go on to Drills B, C and D. You will get the most from each drill if you stop after each one and correct your answers.

Drill 25B

	American Heritage	*Webster*	*Thorndike*
1. joy	_____	_____	_____
2. journey	_____	_____	_____
3. ladle	_____	_____	_____
4. jealous	_____	_____	_____
5. push	_____	_____	_____

Drill 25C

	American Heritage	*Webster*	*Thorndike*
1. hidden	_____	_____	_____
1. view	_____	_____	_____
3. lacquer	_____	_____	_____
4. jaw	_____	_____	_____
5. robbed	_____	_____	_____

Drill 25D

	American Heritage	*Webster*	*Thorndike*
1. lagoon	_____	_____	_____
2. jumbo	_____	_____	_____
3. kitty	_____	_____	_____
4. rear	_____	_____	_____
5. farther	_____	_____	_____

> Remember to add several new words to your personal word list on pages 9 through 13 every time you do a drill; add at least five words per week from your reading.

Section 3

Answer Key

Drill 1: Guide Words

Race 1	Race 2	Race 3
1. 13	1. 26	1. 18
2. 19	2. 22	2. 27
3. 24	3. 10	3. 24
4. 22	4. 18	4. 23
5. 10	5. 24	5. 26
6. 14	6. 16	6. 20
7. 21	7. 19	7. 18
8. 24	8. 10	8. 22
9. 10	9. 13	9. 11
10. 14	10. 24	10. 26

Drill 2: Alphabetizing

Drill 2A

1. careen
2. career
3. carefree
4. careful
5. chipmunk
6. chipper
7. chorus
8. circle
9. circuit
10. citizen

Drill 2: Alphabetizing (continued)

Drill 2B

1. Juneau ↕ jungle ↕ junior

6. judicature ↕ judicial ↕ judiciary

2. kilter ↑ kimono ↑ kin

7. kerchief ↑ kernel ↕ kerosene

3. journalism ↕ journey ↕ journeyman

8. jackpot ↕ jack rabbit ↕ Jackson

4. kennel ↕ Kentucky ↕ Kenya

9. lackluster ↕ laconic ↕ lacquer

5. Ladino ↕ ladle ↕ lady

10. keepsake ↕ keg ↕ Keller

Drill 2C

1. jet engine ↕ jetsam ↕ jettison

6. jurisdiction ↑ jurisprudence ↑ jurist

2. kinsman ↑ kiosk ↕ kip

7. knife ↕ knight ↕ knit

3. knocker ↕ knock-knee ↕ knock out

8. lackadaisical ↑ lackey ↕ lackluster

4. Jones ↕ jonquil ↕ Jonson

9. kite ↕ kith ↕ kitten

5. junket ↕ Juno ↕ junta

10. laity ↕ lake ↑ lam

Drill 3: Multiple Meanings — Homographs

1. **jar²**   To make or utter a harsh sound.

2. **kro·na²**   The basic monetary unit of Sweden.

3. **junk²**   A Chinese flat-bottomed sailing ship.

4. **jade²**   A broken-down horse; nag.

5. **jam¹**   To drive or wedge forcibly; squeeze into a tight position.

6. **kind¹**   Showing sympathy, concern, or understanding.

7. **lam²**   To depart swiftly.

8. **jog¹**   To jolt.

9. **jet¹**   A dense black coal that takes a high polish and is used for jewelry.

10. **kit·ty¹**   A pool or fund of money.

Drill 4: Multiple Meanings — Parts of Speech

Drill 4A	**Drill 4B**
1. noun	1. v.
2. verb	2. n.
3. verb	3. adv.
4. noun	4. adj.
5. adjective	5. v.
6. adverb	6. n.
7. adjective	7. adj.
8. noun	8. n.
9. noun	9. adj.
10. verb	10. adv.

Drill 5: Accent and Alternate Pronunciations

Drill 5A

1. jăk′ĭt
2. jə-lŏp′ē
3. jo͞o′bə-lənt
4. lə-go͞on′
5. kĭn′dər-gärt′n
6. nŏl′ĭj
7. lā′dē-bŭg′
8. jăn′ə-tər
9. jo͞o-dĭsh′əl
10. kăng′gə-ro͞o′

Drill 5B

1. jo͝or′ər, jo͝or′ôr′
2. kēn′yə, kĕn′yə
3. ī′və-rē, iv′rē
4. kĕr′ə-sēn′, kĕr′ə-sēn′
5. jō-hăn′ĭs-bûrg′, yō-hä′nĭs-bûrg′

Drill 5C

1. y, N
2. /y/, O
3. y, N
4. y, N
5. y, N

Drill 6: Syllabication

Drill 6A

1. **jok·er** (jō′kər)
2. **knowl·edge·a·ble** (nŏl′ĭ-jə-bəl)
3. **la·bo·ri·ous** (lə-bôr′ē-əs, lə-bōr′-)
4. **jad·ed** (jā-dĭd)
5. **kid·nap** (kĭd′năp′)
6. **jab·ber** (jăb′ər)
7. **jif·fy** (jĭf′ē)
8. **ken·nel** (kĕn′əl)
9. **land·ing** (lăn′dĭng)
10. **jan·i·tor** (jăn′ə-tər)

Drill 6B

1. **kin·dle** (kĭnd′l)
2. **jo·vi·al** (jō′vē-əl)
3. **jer·kin** (jûr′kən)
4. **kit·ten** (kĭt′n)
5. **jour·nal** (jûr′nəl)
6. **ket·tle** (kĕt′l)
7. **jig·gle** (jĭg′əl)
8. **lad·en** (lād′n)
9. **kitch·en** (kĭch′ən)
10. **kin·der·gar·ten** (kĭn′dər-gärt′n)

Drill 7: Foreign Alphabets

Answers will vary

Drill 8: Idioms and Hyphenated Words

Drill 8A

1. jet engine
2. knock-knee
3. knock out
4. jaw breaker
5. justice of the peace
6. landslide
7. jack rabbit
8. Janus-faced
9. key punch
10. jack-of-all-trades

Drill 8B

1. kettledrum
2. jackknife
3. know-it-all
4. job lot
5. jack-in-the-pulpit
6. lampblack
7. know-how
8. land grant
9. kingpin
10. ivory tower

Drill 9: Prefixes: *Non-* and *Re-*

Drill 9A

1. main entry
2. table
3. table
4. main entry
5. table
6. table
7. main entry
8. table
9. table
10. main entry
11. table
12. main entry

Drill 9B

1. main entry
2. table
3. table
4. main entry
5. table
6. table
7. main entry
8. table
9. main entry
10. table
11. table
12. table

Drill 10: Abbreviations

1. junction

2. knot

3. Joint Chiefs of Staff

4. Los Angeles

5. judge advocate

6. krypton

7. junior varsity

8. karat

9. justice of the peace

10. laboratory

11. kilowatt

12. kitchen police

13. Ku Klux Klan

14. Javanese

15. a. karat

   b. kilo-

   c. Kelvin (temperature scale)

   d. potassium

Drill 11: Etymology

Drill 11A

1. Hebrew

2. French

3. German

4. African

5. Mexican

6. Swedish

7. Tagalog

8. Arabic

9. Russian

10. Yiddish

Drill 11B

1. [< Old English *cnyttan*, to tie in a knot.]

2. [< Greek *lampein*, to shine.]

3. [< Latin *canis*, dog.]

4. [< Old English *hladan*, to load.]

5. [< Greek *kruptos*, hidden.]

6. [< Latin *jūrāta*, thing sworn.]

7. [< Latin *caulis*, cabbage.]

8. [< Old French *jeter*, to throw, project.]

9. [< Old English *cennan*, to make known.]

10. [< Late Greek *iōbēlos*, jubilee.]

Drill 12: Symbols

Drill 12A

1. infinity (or: haze; dust haze)
2. sum
3. take
4. number
5. at
6. copyright
7. angle
8. therefore
9. dieresis
10. Venus (or: female)

Drill 12B

1. $>$
2. $\because$
3. $\pm$
4. $\uparrow$
5. $\div$
6. $\cup$
7. %
8. $\triangleq$
9. $-$
10. $<$

Drill 13: Reference

Drill 13A

1. Genghis Khan
2. 17th President of the U.S.
3. 1929
4. 1826
5. Jupiter
6. 7th
7. Revolutionary War
8. German
9. 1908
10. English poet and dramatist

Drill 13B

1. Somalia, Ethiopia, Sudan, Uganda, Tanzania
2. Nairobi
3. 248,000
4. Nigeria
5. 10
6. Laos
7. Amman
8. Caribbean
9. Sudan
10. 1,296,000

Drill 14: Consonants

Drill 14A

1. /z/	9. /s/
2. /s/	10. /s/
3. /z/	11. /z/
4. /s/	12. /z/
5. /s/	13. /s/
6. /s/	14. /s/
7. /s/	15. /z/
8. /z/	

Drill 14B

1. /k/	9. /k/
2. /k/	10. /s/
3. /k/	11. /k/
4. /s/	12. /k/
5. /k/	13. /k/
6. /k/	14. /k/
7. /s/	15. /k/
8. /s/	

Drill 15: Short and Long Vowels

Drill 15A

1. nŏt
2. hōme
3. hŏt
4. stŏp
5. hōpe
6. pŏp
7. alōne
8. sō
9. clŏck
10. hellō

Drill 15B

1. hăd
2. băck
3. māde
4. bāby
5. ăs
6. ăfter
7. rādio
8. lăst
9. āble
10. ănd

Drill 15C

1. ĕgg
2. shē
3. ĕxtra
4. bē
5. thĕn
6. gĕt
7. lēgal
8. rēbound
9. ēqual
10. ĕdit

Drill 15D

1. ĭnto
2. fīve
3. ĭf
4. ĭnch
5. rīde
6. dĭd
7. thĭs
8. tīny
9. whĭch
10. pīlot

Drill 15E

1. ŭs
2. ŭnder
3. bŭt
4. rŭn
5. mŭch
6. jŭst

Drill 16: Rules for Long Vowels

Drill 16A

1. sō
2. hŏt
3. fŏx
4. clŏck
5. gō
6. drŏp

Drill 16B

1. hŏt
2. bŏdy
3. hōmé
4. jōké
5. drŏp
6. stōné
7. glōbé
8. pŏp
9. măt
10. māté
11. līké
12. dĭd

Drill 16C: Review

1. ŭp — closed-syllable
2. nōsé — final e
3. shē — open-syllable
4. cāmé — final e
5. whīté — final e
6. ĕgg — closed-syllable
7. lăst — closed-syllable
8. fīvé — final e
9. bĭt — closed-syllable
10. bīté — final e
11. gō — open-syllable
12. bē — open-syllable
13. lōné — final e
14. stăsh — closed-syllable
15. mŏm — closed-syllable
16. pōpé — final e
17. sŭp — closed-syllable
18. hī — open-syllable
19. dŏt — closed-syllable
20. pōlé — final e

Drill 16D

1. /ē/
2. /y/
3. /ē/
4. /y/
5. /ī/
6. /y/
7. /ē/
8. /y/
9. /ē/
10. /ī/
11. /y/
12. /ī/
13. /ē/
14. /y/
15. /ē/
16. /ī/
17. /y/
18. /ē/
19. /ī/
20. /ē/

Drill 17: Difficult Consonants

Drill 17A

1. jŏng′kwĭl   / kw /

2. jĭngks   / ks /

3. kŭm′kwŏt′   / kw /

4. jŭk′stə-pōz′   / ks /

Drill 17B

1. / ks /	13. / kw /
2. / kw /	14. / g /
3. / j /	15. / g /
4. / j /	16. / j /
5. / ks /	17. / g /
6. / j /	18. / kw /
7. / g /	19. / ks /
8. / ks /	20. / g /
9. / kw /	21. / ks /
10. / ks /	22. / j /
11. / kw /	23. / kw /
12. / j /	24. / j /

Drill 17C

1. / *th* /	13. / *th* /
2. / th /	14. / th /
3. / *th* /	15. / sh /
4. / ch /	16. / hw /
5. / th /	17. / *th* /
6. / sh /	18. / ch /
7. / hw /	19. / hw /
8. / sh /	20. / sh /
9. / ch /	21. / *th* /
10. / *th* /	22. / sh /
11. / hw /	23. / ch /
12. / ch /	24. / th /

Drill 18: Schwa and Long Vowel Digraphs

Drill 18A

1. e
2. a
3. a
4. a
5. a
6. i
7. e
8. o
9. o
10. a
11. e
12. a

Drill 18B

1. /ə/
2. /ŏ/
3. /ə/
4. /ə/
5. /ă/
6. /ə/
7. /ə/
8. /ĭ/
9. /ă/
10. /ĕ/

Drill 18C

1. /ĕ/
2. /ē/
3. /ē/
4. /ā/
5. /ā/
6. /ĕ/
7. /ē/
8. /ā/
9. /ō/
10. /ē/
11. /ā/
12. /ā/
13. /ō/
14. /ō/
15. /ou/
16. /ou/
17. /ō/
18. /ĕ/
19. /ē/
20. /ā/
21. /ē/
22. /ā/
23. /ā/
24. /ĕ/
25. /ē/
26. /ō/
27. /ē/
28. /ō/
29. /ō/
30. /ou/

Drill 18D:
Review

1. /ə/
2. /ŏ/
3. /ou/
4. /ā/
5. /ə/
6. /ĕ/
7. /ō/
8. /ə/
9. /ē/
10. /ă/
11. /ā/
12. /ə/
13. /ē/
14. /ĭ/
15. /ə/
16. /ə/
17. /ō/
18. /ĭ/
19. /ə/
20. /ā/
21. /ə/
22. /ou/
23. /ă/
24. /ə/
25. /ĕ/
26. /ō/
27. /ə/
28. /ŏ/
29. /ē/
30. /ĕ/

Drill 19: *R*-modified Vowels

Drill: 19A

1. /ûr/	11. /ûr/
2. /ûr/	12. /ôr/
3. /är/	13. /âr/
4. /ôr/	14. /ûr/
5. /ûr/	15. /är/
6. /ûr/	16. /är/
7. /är/	17. /ûr/
8. /âr/	18. /ôr/
9. /ôr/	19. /âr/
10. /âr/	20. /ûr/

Drill 19B: Review

1. /ûr/	11. /ôr/
2. /är/	12. /ā/
3. /ē/	13. /ō/
4. /ûr/	14. /ûr/
5. /ō/	15. /âr/
6. /ûr/	16. /ā/
7. /âr/	17. /ûr/
8. /är/	18. /är/
9. /ē/	19. /âr/
10. /ûr/	20. /ûr/

Drill 20: Broad *O*

Drill 20: Review

1. /ô/	7. /ō/	13. /ō/	19. /ŏ/
2. /ō/	8. /ō/	14. /ô/	20. /ō/
3. /ə/	9. /ô/	15. /ŏ/	21. /ō/
4. /ō/	10. /ŏ/	16. /ô/	22. /ō/
5. /ō/	11. /ə/	17. /ô/	23. /ŏ/
6. /ô/	12. /ō/	18. /ō/	24. /ō/
			25. /ŏ/

Drill 21: Diphthongs and Review of *A* Sounds

Drill 21A

1. /oi/
2. /oi/
3. /ou/
4. /ou/
5. /ou/
6. /oi/
7. /ō/
8. /oi/
9. /ou/
10. /oi/
11. /ou/
12. /ō/
13. /oi/
14. /ou/
15. /oi/
16. /ou/
17. /oi/
18. /ou/
19. /ō/
20. /ou/

**Drill 21B:
Review**

1. /ā/
2. /ā/
3. /ă/
4. /ā/
5. /ă/
6. /ā/
7. /ə/
8. /ā/
9. /ā/
10. /ă/
11. /ā/
12. /är/
13. /ə/
14. /ā/
15. /ə/
16. /âr/
17. /ā/
18. /ə/
19. /âr/
20. /är/

Drill 22: Sounds of *OO*

Drill 22A

1. /ŏŏ/
2. /ŏŏ/
3. /ōō/
4. /ōō/
5. /ōō/
6. /ŏŏ/
7. /ŏŏ/
8. /ōō/
9. /ōō/
10. /ŏŏ/

Drill 22B

1. /ŏŏ/
2. /ōō/
3. /ōō/
4. /ōō/
5. /ŏŏ/
6. /ŏŏ/
7. /ōō/
8. /ōō/
9. /ŏŏ/
10. /ōō/

Drill 22: Sounds of *OO* (continued)

Drill 22C

1. /ŏo/
2. /o͞o/
3. /ûr/
4. /o͞o/
5. /ŭ/
6. /o͞o/
7. /o͞o/
8. /ō/
9. /o͞o/
10. /ŏo/
11. /ûr/
12. /o͞o/
13. /ŏo/
14. /ŭ/
15. /o͞o/

Drill 22D

1. /yo͞o/
2. /o͞o/
3. /o͞o/
4. /yo͞o/
5. /o͞o/
6. /yo͞o/
7. /o͞o/
8. /o͞o/
9. /yo͞o/
10. /o͞o

Drill 23: Consonant Blends and Phonograms

1. sick
   stick
   pick

2. bought
   thought
   fought

3. fight
   sight
   slight

4. sound
   found
   ground

5. sore
   more
   store

6. catch
   hatch
   thatch

7. rock
   sock
   dock

8. fold
   mold
   sold

9. bleak
   speak
   streak

10. snack
    pack
    rack

11. hip
    snip
    drip

12. sob
    rob
    knob

13. loop
    coop
    troop

14. slow
    know
    tow

Drill 24: Exceptions

Drill 24A

1. /f/
2. /—/
3. /—/
4. /ng/
5. /zh/
6. /ng/
7. /—/
8. /zh/
9. /—/
10. /—/

Drill 24B

1. /zh/
2. /—/
3. /—/
4. /—/
5. /—/
6. /—/
7. /zh/
8. /—/
9. /f/
10. /—/
11. /zh/
12. /ng/
13. /—/
14. /—/
15. /ng/
16. /—/
17. /—/
18. /f/
19. /—/
20. /—/

Drill 25: Comparing Other Dictionary Phonetic Systems

Drill 25A

	American Heritage	*Webster*	*Thorndike*
1.	foul	faùl	foul
2.	băk	bak	bak
3.	jŭg	jəg	jug
4.	jō͞o′sē	jü′sē	jü′sē
5.	shâr	sheər	sher, shar

Drill 25B

	American Heritage	Webster	Thorndike
1.	joi	jȯi	joi
2.	jûr′nē	jər′nē	jėr′nē
3.	lād′l	lād′l	lā′dl
4.	jĕl′əs	jel′əs	jel′əs
5.	poŏsh	pu̇sh	pu̇sh

Drill 25C

	American Heritage	Webster	Thorndike
1.	hĭd′n	hid′n	hid′n
2.	vyo͞o	vyü	vyü
3.	lăk′ər	lak′ər	lak′ər
4.	jô	jȯ	jô
5.	rŏbd	räbd	robd

Drill 25D

	American Heritage	Webster	Thorndike
1.	lə-go͞on′	lə-gün′	lə-gün′
2.	jŭm′bō	jəm′bō	jum′bō
3.	kĭt′ē	kit′ē	kit′ē
4.	rîr	riər	rir
5.	fär′thər	fär′thər	fär′ᵮHər